Criminal Justice
Recent Scholarship

Edited by
Marilyn McShane and Frank P. Williams III

A Series from LFB Scholarly

Police Requests for Compliance
Coercive and Procedurally Just Tactics

John D. McCluskey

LFB Scholarly Publishing LLC
New York 2003

Library of Congress Cataloging-in-Publication Data

McCluskey, John D. (John David), 1969-
  Police requests for compliance : coercive and procedurally just
tactics / John D. McCluskey.
        p. cm. -- (Criminal justice)
  Includes bibliographical references and index.
  ISBN 1-931202-61-3 (alk. paper)
  1. Police patrol. 2. Police-community relations. 3. Compliance. I.
Title. II. Criminal justice (LFB Scholarly Publishing LLC)
  HV8080.P2M33 2003
  363.2'3--dc21

2003009017

ISBN 1-931202-61-3

Printed on acid-free 250-year-life paper.

Manufactured in the United States of America.

Table of Contents

Acknowledgement

Regardless of whether a single author is listed, an extensive research project is never conducted alone. Mentors, colleagues, and family have all contributed immensely to the completion of this research.

Robert Worden, Stephen Mastrofski, and Roger Parks, who along with Albert Reiss, Jr. were principal investigators on the Project on Policing Neighborhoods (POPN), have each made valuable comments, criticisms, and observations that helped to shape the research questions in this book. The POPN project and parts of this research were supported by Grant number 95-IJ-CX-0071 from the National Institute of Justice. Timothy Bynum provided valuable support while I conducted portions of this research at Michigan State University. David Duffee, David McDowall, Hans Toch, and Alissa Worden also provided commentary, suggestions, and criticism that made the final product much better.

My colleagues, William Terrill, Eugene Paoline, and Stephanie Myers also served as important sources of inspiration and encouragement. Justin Patchin helped tremendously by carefully coding narratives and entering data.

Most importantly my wife Cynthia, and our daughters, Liliana and Olivia, have been patient and supportive inspirations. Cynthia Perez McCluskey did double duty, since she also tirelessly edited and improved both the style and substance of the book. I am grateful to all who have given their assistance along the way.

INTRODUCTION

In the existing police literature the examination of police-citizen interaction is largely focused on police actions in dealing with citizens as the outcome or dependent variable (e.g., Smith and Visher, 1981; Smith, 1986; Worden 1989; Mastrofski, Snipes, Parks, and Maxwell, 2000; Novak, Frank, Smith, and Engle, 2002). Citizen behavior and characteristics have been taken into account as *explanations* of police actions and tactics. Research on factors that predict arrest include, for example, citizen's demeanor. Demeanor, by some measures, includes actions that citizens take in the course of police-citizen encounters (see Klinger, 1994; Worden and Shepard, 1995; and Worden, Shepard, and Mastrofski, 1996).

A relatively new approach to examining the dynamics of police-citizen interactions is to focus on citizen actions as a dependent variable (McIver and Parks, 1983). Mastrofski, Snipes, and Supina's (1996) work involving the Richmond police department represents seminal research that moves the study of criminal justice toward explaining the actions of clients and not just actors. The focus of the present research is on a citizen's decision to comply with police requests. Compliance with two kinds of police requests are examined in this study: police requests for identification and police requests for citizen self-control.

Studying the response of citizens to criminal justice is an important task for understanding *how* a criminal justice system works both in a theoretical sense, and for making informed policy decisions. Theoretically, criminal justice often draws on deterrence as the rationale for operating procedures, however, the linkage between various practices and the production of lower crime rates appears tenuous (Bayley, 1998: Introduction). Hence, to understand what

1

works in criminal justice, one would benefit from examining the clients of the system and their reaction to regulation in various forms. Recent research on domestic violence indicates that a variety of mechanisms for regulating citizen behavior produce varying outcomes as client behavior is traced over time (Dunford, Huizinga, and Elliot, 1990; Paternoster et al., 1997). By examining the clients of criminal justice and attempting to model their behavioral outcomes through regulation within the system, researchers may be able to enhance the understanding of the processes that produce differing outcomes. Although deterrence is a parsimonious theory to predict client behavior, new concepts are being added to the mix regarding how the system works in producing individual outcomes (Braithwaite, 1989; Sherman, 1993; Tyler, 1990).

One advance in the study of criminal justice processing is the research on compliance as a social phenomenon. Examinations of compliance, in a general sense, are focused on the *outcome* of a request that a target do X. Hence, the phenomenon has wide ranging implications: Countries can be requested to comply with international regulations, corporations can comply (or not) with administrative regulations, and children can comply (or not) with their parents' requests to behave (Hawkins, 1983; Henkin, 1979; Patterson, et al. 1992). The thread that binds these diverse examples is an actor's request that a target adjust its behavior in line with the actor's stated desire.

The issue of compliance with authoritative requests spans several fields of inquiry: Political psychologists question how legitimacy and hierarchy influence obedience (Milgram, 1973; Tyler, 1990), social theorists raise questions about how "cultural" differences affect obedience (Lanza-Kaduce and Greenleaf, 1994), and from the psychological perspective researchers ponder what situational and attitudinal textures predict compliance (Tedeschi and Felson, 1994). Compliance with rules has been examined in the context of regulatory bodies enforcing administrative law (Hawkins, 1983; Makkai and Braithwaite, 1994). Studies of compliance have examined settings as diverse as litigant behavior in paying settlements (McEwen and Maiman, 1984) and children's compliance with parental rules (Patterson, Reid, and Dishion, 1992). General statements regarding compliance have not yet been generated, since the concept concerns a diverse phenomenon (Brehm, 1996). Issues of compliance are an emergent component of criminal justice research.

Recently, the issue of compliance has been explored in the context of police-citizen interactions (Mastrofski, Snipes, and Supina, 1996). To address compliance as a topic of study in criminal justice, this study is reversing the typical inquiry in that field, which is the explanation of police, prosecutor, parole officer, or other criminal justice agent's exercise of discretion. The exercise of discretion by criminal justice actors has long been the central focus of scholarship in the field (Gottfredson and Gottfredson, 1980; Walker, 1992). With respect to policing this observation is particularly true. The current study of compliance, however, focuses on the citizen, or client, as a decision-maker.

Identifying the factors that influence citizen decisions to obey is at the core of this research. The theoretical frameworks used to predict citizens' compliant behavior have been sharpened by theoretical integration and empirical examination (Paternoster et al., 1997; Sherman, 1993). A mixture of theoretical approaches will be used to model the calculus that citizens use in determining whether to obey or rebel. If we can expand the knowledge of what generates obedience and rebellion among clients, the criminal justice system can redefine its tactics and strategies to comport with predictive factors. For instance, the *legitimacy* of criminal justice intervention is likely to have an effect on the target's reaction to regulation. The concept of legitimacy has a history of theoretical importance in explaining successful regulation (e.g., Toch, 1969). Recently, empirical examinations of legitimacy and compliance have explicitly linked the quality of police treatment (as an indicator of legitimacy) and subsequent citizen behavior (Mastrofski et al., 1996; McCluskey, Mastrofski, Parks, 1999; Paternoster et al., 1997). Further exploring this linkage will offer insight into the decision making processes of clients and aid police managers in identifying strategies and tactics that will increase compliance.

In particular, this study aims to elaborate upon the theoretical framework informing both Mastrofski and colleagues (1996) and McCluskey et al. (1999). Both studies found that indicators of legitimacy, among others, are important in predicting citizens' decisions to comply. Herein it is argued that more precise measures and more specific hypotheses must be brought to bear on the issue of compliance to achieve two closely related goals. First, the current study will identify police actions that impact citizens' decisions to comply. To that end we attempt to answer questions such as: What strategies for handling interpersonal conflicts lead to higher incidence of compliance, when holding all else equal? Second, this research will attempt to explore the relative success of police tactics that bring the rebellious citizens into conformance.

This study examines citizen compliance as a phenomenon whose explanation requires the understanding of the immediate contours of the police-citizen encounter as well as the context within which that encounter is embedded. We argue that a combination of officer actions (e.g., use of threats), situational factors (e.g. presence of bystanders), and the context provided by geographic setting (e.g. levels of concentrated disadvantage) are vital for predicting compliance. The remainder of this book explores compliance as a predictable phenomenon, examines situational variables that are hypothesized to impact compliance, develops hypotheses regarding the effect of contextual factors on compliance, describes the data and methods that are used to model the phenomenon, and reports the findings of those analyses.

COMPLIANCE AS A GENERAL PHENOMENON

To begin a reasoned discussion and empirical examination of any phenomenon the concept must be definable (Gibbs, 1981: preface, 110). The term "compliance" and those who study the phenomenon, represent a disparate set of disciplines and questions. Brehm's (1996) discourse on the diversity of the notion of compliance concludes that any general statement concerning the concept requires hypotheses that would bridge wide-ranging phenomena. As a general statement we propose the opportunity for compliance to be present when an authority requests that a target perform a stated task or refrain from engaging in a specific behavior. The request could have a variety of forms, including legislative statutes, administrative rules, and verbal statements.

Social scientists have studied compliance in diverse settings (family processes, taxpaying behavior), and it would be useful to survey some of this previous research to understand the nature of the phenomenon to be studied. The survey of the literature will give greater breadth, depth, and understanding to the multifaceted nature of compliance. For the sake of clarity we will first briefly introduce the range of situations in which one could study compliance. Second, we will explore the commonalities that exist in studying compliance across social settings. Third, we will address the differences that exist across these settings. Finally, we will argue for the development of hypotheses specific to police-citizen encounters.

EXAMPLES OF COMPLIANCE

Compliance can be examined as a phenomenon that exists across states (Brehm, 1996). At the international level one could study whether a nation fully complies with the terms of a treaty. Compliance can also be examined within organizational hierarchies. A leader's overt attempt to change the work habits of an employee and the response to that effort would be, by nature of our broad definition, an example of a compliance situation. The work of Tyler and Degoey (1996) exemplifies research framed around employee compliance (see also Wagner and Moriarty, 2002; Lambert, 2003; for application to criminal justice settings). Compliance, or rather, adherence research is also an important part of medical trials examining the effectiveness of drugs and other treatment regimens. Whether a patient is willing to maintain a diet, take a daily dose of medicine, or reduce risky behavior at the behest of a doctor are widely studied compliance phenomena (Pendelton, 1983). Another form of such individual-individual research on compliance would be Patterson et al.'s youth training models (1992). That research examines various parenting techniques for gaining compliance from the targeted child.

The area of compliance on which researchers in criminal justice and criminology tend to focus is that of State-Individual relations or citizen compliance with law (Brehm, 1996). This nexus allows for numerous opportunities for compliance research. For example, McEwen and Maiman (1984) examined the nature of citizen's compliance with court ordered settlements in small claims courts in Maine. Casey and Scholz (1995) examined taxpayer compliance with the tax code. Scholz and Pinney (1995) as well as Klepper and Nagin (1989) have also conducted research on the determinants of tax compliance.

SIMILARITIES ACROSS COMPLIANCE PHENOMENA

Regardless of the status of the requestor (parent, nation, police officer) and the target (child, nation, suspect) there are similarities among compliance situations. The most salient dimensions with regard to this research, we argue, are the authority of the requestor and the existence of a power base that is used to make a target comply (See Brehm, 1996 for an alternate conception and discussion). Authority represents the ability of the requestor to exercise control over the subject (e.g., Arendt, 1973). In each of the cases delineated above, the requestor has authority to make a request of the target, at least in some imagined scenarios for each type. In all of the situations discussed thus far, the requestor has had authority when paired with the target. Such authority-subject relationships make for a common dimension on which to study compliance requests as a homogenous phenomenon.

Power, as distinguished from authority, represents the ability of the requestor to enforce his or her will on a resistant target (e.g., Klockars, 1984). The IRS can bring coercive power against taxpayers, nations can threaten other nations with military might, police can coerce citizens with legal and physical force, and so on. It is also true that the targets of coercion can resist the force that is used to move them to a compliant position. This dimension permeates all cases of compliance. A requestor must have the power to influence the resistant target. The dimensions of authority and power represent the most salient commonalities among targets and requestors. A requestor has the authority to make a demand or request of the target and both actors can use a power base to manipulate the outcome of the confrontation between the two parties.

DIFFERENCES IN COMPLIANCE PHENOMENA

In the following section we specify some dimensions where compliance situations, which are ubiquitous in human interaction, are distinguished from one another. Brehm (1996) has argued that there are similarities across compliance situations and has argued for the creation of a general model that explains compliance. The identification of compliance across situations does not necessarily facilitate the creation of a general theory of compliance. Rather, one would benefit from exploring the differences that exist in compliance situations. In examining the literature on taxpayer compliance, regulatory compliance, patient compliance with treatment regimens, and children's compliance with parental requests we argue that there are important differences when compared to citizen compliance in the police-citizen encounter. We use the following dimensions to contrast the differences in compliance situations between police and citizens as compared with other target-requestor relationships: *power bases* on which requestors most typically rely, *proximity* of target and requestor, *transience* of the target-requestor relationship, and how targets gain *admission status* in the compliance game.

Within the exploration of similarities we have unintentionally broached a subtle difference that exists between the various compliance situations, which is the *power base* on which the requestor draws. French and Raven (1959) delineated a series of power bases including reward, coercive, legitimate, referent, and expert power. A comparison of police-suspect interaction and doctor-patient interaction, for example, would indicate that on one level, power is important in gaining compliance. If, however, one were to analyze the interactions of these two dyads it would be clear that the police would be more likely to rely on a *coercive* power base and the doctor would likely rely on an *expert* power base in goading the target into acquiescing. Thus, even within an apparent similarity, that of the use of power, we find that compliance situations vary.

Proximity is the distance of the requestor from the compliance target. In cases of regulatory agencies, taxpayer compliance, and treaty compliance, the requestor is a faceless government. Agency inspections, audits, and international inspections require the commitment of an individual or group requestor to establish whether the target is in compliance. Conversely, in situations involving police-citizen contact, doctor-patient contact, or parent-child interaction, compliance can be studied as a face-to-face human interaction. The ability to monitor behavior of the target in such encounters is more viable, but depends on the nature of the requested behavior. Police, parents, and doctors can measure target behavior against an instantly articulated standard. Compliance encounters involving closer *proximity* are more amenable to being studied as instances of social interaction. Adherence to regulatory restrictions, the tax code, or international treaties lacks the immediacy of contact between target and requestor. In instances of interpersonal contact, requestors and targets can manipulate the immediate social environment to gain acquiescence or resist a request by emanating social cues to the other interactant.

Transience refers to the duration of the target-requestor relationship. Targets such as businesses, which are accountable to regulatory agencies as requestors, often have long and cooperative histories with authorities (Hawkins, 1983). Regardless of *quality*, the parent-child relationship is also one with a history (and is likely to persist into the future) from which both actors can draw information in a compliance game. Doctors can have long relationships with patients in which they can experiment with various approaches to gaining compliance with treatment regimens. The police-citizen encounter, by contrast, is a fleeting interaction (Sykes and Brent, 1983). The stability of the aforementioned examples does not exist within the police-citizen dyad. Where cues pass between the target and requestor on a regular basis a routine of interaction is likely to develop, moreover, compliance may be affected by the target's anticipated interaction with the requestor. Such a familiar sequence is especially unlikely for the citizen who is placed in the role of victim or suspect (Sykes and Brent, 1983).[1]

Admission status into the compliance game can be voluntary or involuntary. Patients visit doctors and assent to be treated for their conditions. The voluntary doctor-patient relationship has been termed "paternalism with permission" (Cross and Churchill, 1982). Similarly, nations can enter into cooperative treaties with other nations for mutual self-defense (Patchin, 1988). In both instances the target is volunteering cooperation in exchange for self-interest, such as the alleviation of pain. Clearly taxpayers, businesses within the sphere of an agency's regulatory mandate, and the citizen within the police-citizen encounter are less voluntary participants.[2] Police encounters with suspects, in particular, represent a contact where target *admission status* is clearly involuntary. Where doctor-patient relationships can grow based on cooperation, trust, and compatibility of interests the police-citizen (especially suspect-police) relationship is adversarial and likely to be based on incompatible interests. The police possess power to intervene in emergencies and *impose* solutions to handle situational exigencies (Bittner, 1970).

While power bases, proximity, transience, and admission status do not completely describe the differences between various requestor-target dyads it is sufficient to distinguish police-citizen encounters as a unique form of the more general compliance phenomenon. Police can legitimately draw on *coercive* power to obtain compliance (Bittner, 1970), have a close proximity to the target in street level encounters, the encounters are transient in nature, and citizens, especially suspects, typically have an involuntary admission status in the compliance game. Other compliance situations can inform the present research, but hypotheses regarding the causes of compliant target behavior require sensitivity to the singular nature of police-citizen encounters. To explain compliance in police-citizen encounters we will draw largely on literature incorporating human interaction, justice concerns, and the location of events in geographic space. Predictors that might explain other forms of compliance, but which are unlikely to be useful to us herein will be ignored in the remainder of this book.

COMPLIANCE AND CRIMINAL JUSTICE RESEARCH

Compliance is an important phenomenon in the context of criminal justice because it reflects the State's ability to enforce the law without directly relying on the coercive power of *formal* sanction. Compliance with the law is quasi-voluntary, or in the parlance of McEwen and Maiman (1984) it is said to require consent in some form. Research on regulatory agencies indicates that voluntary compliance is regarded as a superior method of regulation (see Braithwaite, 1989; Hawkins, 1983; Makkai and Braithwaite, 1994). If compliance can be accomplished short of a state intervening coercively, resources can be conserved. Beyond fiscal soundness, one could argue that compliance strategies represent an evolutionary step towards a pacifistic form of governance (Bittner, 1970; cf. Back, 1983).

This study examines citizen acquiescence to police requests. As previously stated, this is a departure from typical theoretical discourses and empirical analyses in criminal justice which focus largely on police behavior and use citizen characteristics and actions as predictors. Requests for compliance represents a middle range tactic between doing nothing or ignoring the suspect, and making an arrest that police may invoke to "handle" situations (Berk and Loseke, 1981).[3] The success of such tactics is largely unexplored in a literature that is preoccupied with predicting the decision to arrest (Worden, 1989).

The police literature indicates that arrests are frequently *not made* in situations where they would be legally justifiable (Berk and Loseke, 1981; Brown, 1988). In cases involving disputes, for instance, alternative tactics are used to "handle" the situation (Bayley, 1986; Black, 1980; and Berk and Loseke, 1981). Police observation indicates that informal solutions to problems dominate the modal tour of a police officer and the formal invocation of the law is a rare event (Reiss, 1971).

It is an oversimplification to limit police tactics to arrest or inaction. Instead, the police often adopt the middle range tactics that

Bayley (1986) observed in the Denver, Colorado police department and Black (1980) observed in Chicago, Washington, and Boston. Mediation, negotiation, and informal settlement of problems is a common response of law enforcement officers to situations that are within the ambit of formal legal action (Brown, 1988: Chapter 7; Muir, 1977). Part of learning the "craft" of policing is learning the judicious use of the law and other resources to solve problems (Bayley and Bittner, 1984). Muir's (1977) exploration of officer styles illustrates how these craftsmen develop operational routines by contrasting the styles of the "enforcer" and the "professional" in dealing with domestic cases. The professional officer, in Muir's opinion, is more apt to opt for an informal reconnection of tattered social bonds, than invoke the law as a mechanism to handle the situation.

A request for compliance, if defined as a mechanism less formal than arrest, represents a middle range tool between inaction and invoking formal sanctions at the disposal of criminal justice actors. Requests that citizens correct their offending behavior, especially with respect to disputes, is a common action taken by police (Bayley, 1986; Black, 1980). Researchers concerned with administrative rule enforcement have identified compliance as a powerful regulatory tool when used 'correctly' (see Hawkins, 1983; Makkai and Braithwaite, 1994). We argue that the examination of police requests for compliance and citizen responses to such requests would be a valuable contribution to criminal justice. More generally, the target's response to such requests, when used in police-citizen encounters, is a case of informal regulation that requires investigation.

The study of compliance in police-citizen encounters will rely on the interactive nature of police-citizen contacts. As citizen behavior is used to predict police behaviors (Worden, 1989), this research relies on police actions as predictors of citizen decisions. The hypotheses developed below are based largely on social interactionist theory, which emphasizes the reciprocity of human behavior. This proposed examination of citizens/clients as decision-makers represents the next step in exploring how the justice system operates at the street level. This endeavor requires that we first develop a theory of compliance.

CHAPTER 1

EXPLAINING COMPLIANCE

Compliance is an increasingly important tool for police as they depart from the "crime-fighting" and legalistic roles promulgated by police professionalization (e.g., Reiss, 1984). To understand this phenomenon in the context of police-citizen encounters this study adopts a framework that builds upon Mastrofski and colleagues (1996) and McCluskey et al. (1999). Compliance models specified in the aforementioned research include nearly thirty predictors of citizen compliance drawing on conflict theory, police wisdom, social interactionist theory, and social bondedness as sources of hypotheses. Using this research as a starting point we note that the social interactionist perspective is especially significant for generating hypotheses for predicting compliance. Arguments against the inclusion of conflict theory and police wisdom in the current research are then presented.

This study focuses largely on refining hypotheses from the social interactionist perspective, sharpening the procedural justice component used in previous research, and examining the police-citizen encounters as a microsocial process. In the next two chapters we will build a model of compliance centered on procedural justice and social interaction in police-citizen encounters. A second level of inquiry, involving social disorganization theory, will also be adopted to explore the contextual effects of geographic space on citizen actions.

SOCIAL INTERACTIONIST THEORY

The theoretical framework informing this research is drawn largely from the literature generated by social psychologists. Social interactionist theory is used to construct hypotheses regarding citizens' responses to police actions and the interplay of behaviors (Tedeschi and

Felson, 1994:266-267). Research and theory involving procedural justice is also useful to construct hypotheses regarding police and citizen actions, and the outcome of the police-citizen encounter. The primary hypotheses that guide this investigation are explored in the following sections on social interactionist theory and procedural justice.

Social interactionist theory, in accordance with exchange theory, indicates that human interaction is partially based in costs and rewards, or instrumental considerations. Citizen cooperation is likely to be forthcoming when the costs of noncompliance are so great as to be a "deterrent" to rebellion. Conversely, when costs or stakes are perceived to be low compliance is likely to be less prevalent. The "costs" are subjective and vary according to citizen's attitudes regarding what is important. A citizen may believe that her autonomy is very important and be defiant; another may believe that his time is important and comply as a mechanism to limit the cost of the police-citizen encounter. Ideally a researcher would need to understand a citizen's values and cognitions before one could make a prediction or a hypothetical statement regarding what "causes" a citizen to comply. There are two reasons why this approach is neither feasible nor necessary.

First, knowledge of citizen's attitudes in the course of the encounter is unattainable and requires post event interviewing to be captured. This seems to be unreliable in sorting out temporal ordering for what citizens apprehend as important in formulating a decision calculus. Observed behavior is not necessarily linked to attitudes (Azjen, 1987; also see Back, 1983). Furthermore, unobtrusive observation of human interaction does not allow an observer to ask parties questions regarding attitudes, feelings, or thought processes. The crux of interactionist theorizing is that people respond to the actions of *the other*. The effect attitudes might have on interaction is that they could act as a filter which shapes one's perception and interpretation of another's actions. Thus persons with X attitude could systematically interpret an action differently from those who possess Y attitude. While plausible, we argue that this hypothetical connection between attitudes and behavior is not a reason to abandon analysis of human interaction without knowledge of an interactant's attitudes. Furthermore, the police are not operating in a capacity where they know a citizen's attitudinal valence regarding "stakes" in a situation, beyond what a citizen verbalizes. Hence, our "knowing" citizens' psychological evaluation of costs represents a departure from the knowledge an officer has at his or her disposal. We argue that costs and rewards must be represented through concrete, observable events and situational factors. Costs and rewards represent, in this study, elements that are hypothesized to affect a citizen's decision to comply and we assume that these are weighed similarly by citizens. Social interactionist theory is rooted in the interpretation of action and reaction by social actors. It is not crafted specifically for the generation of hypotheses regarding police-citizen interaction, however, it does provide insight with respect to human tendencies to react to various stimuli. This book is consistent with previous work on citizen compliance which has drawn heavily from the theorizing of Tedeschi and Felson (1994). The hypotheses that follow attempt to develop a more precise relationship between police actions and citizen responses than has been previously offered in models explaining citizen compliance with police requests. Of special importance is the police's initial "self-presentation" to the citizen (Goffman, 1959). The importance of police audience will be discussed in the following section on coercion.

COERCION

The coercive balance of power is an integral component of the social interactionist's theoretical framework for understanding human behavior. The coercive balance of power refers to an actor's ability to bring force against another actor. One would argue that the police have a reserve of power by virtue of the coercion inherent in that social role (Bittner, 1970; Klockars, 1984). The authority-subject roles are relatively constant across police-citizen encounters. The use of coercion, however, varies across compliance events and interactants. Some events require requestors use only verbal suggestion for resolutions, others require verbal coercion and cajoling, some require threats backed with legal consequences, and others still require physical contact in order to attain compliance. Similarly, targets can resist requestors with a variety of coercive actions. We will immediately address the coercive power of the requestor, but reserve a discussion of targets' coercive power when we address other attributes of citizens.

Varying types of coercive power represent tools that police have in their arsenals for maintaining control over situations (Muir, 1977; Sykes and Brent, 1983; Van Maanen, 1978). The components of coercion that we are most interested in are arrests, handcuffing, searching, using physical force, and verbal threats to invoke the law or impose physical restraint. In a broad sense these represent the larger domain of physical and verbal control. Additionally, one should also consider the "level" of coercion embedded within the police request, which is likely to lie on a continua from suggestion to overt threatening.

As noted above, the police maintain an authoritative relationship with the citizens with whom they have contact. This permits them to take coercive actions against the citizen to restore order to situations and to deliver justice to aggrieved parties. Exercise of coercion, from a social interactionist perspective, *ceteris paribus*, is hypothesized to increase the probability of compliance of a citizen-target. The citizen who is confronted with more forceful "self-presentation" by the police will be more likely to comply. This formulation suffers from the problem of causal reciprocity: Those citizens who initially resist are likely to have more coercive force used against them. Absent controlling for noncompliance, testing the use of coercion is problematic if force and coercion are distributed in a sample according to citizen resistance. Thus we argue that an added component of theoretical importance is the citizen's initial action toward the police. Both actors emit an initial self-presentation that is, for our purposes, a starting point for determining future actions and reactions.

The importance of entry tactics in shaping the trajectory of the encounter is made clear through Bayley's (1986) initial examination of tactical choices and, in the more specific case of compliance, Mastrofski and colleagues' (1996) work, which explicitly linked forceful entry and citizen's choice to obey.[1] Entry tactics are important because they set the tone for the entire encounter and are analogous to the "initial state" of a dynamic process (Sykes and Brent, 1983). As mothers often say, "you never get a second chance to make a first impression" or in the parlance of social interactionists, the impression that is projected is likely to hang on this initial presentation of self that police display to the compliance target (Goffman, 1959). The interaction between citizen and officer is "conditioned" by this initial state. Whether an officer enters a situation with no force, verbal force, physical force, or by asking a question is likely to be have a lasting effect on the citizen's perception of the situation, future responses to the officer, and the future actions of both parties. Forceful entry may encourage resistance and set the tone for the subsequent *danse macabre* between the police and the citizen. Police wisdom, as noted by Mastrofski and colleagues (1996), is divided on the predictive power of entry tactics. Some argue that the forceful entry cuts off an opportunity for resistance, others advocate a measured entrance that allows officers to "ratchet up" coercion as necessary to gain citizen obedience. The initial state of an encounter is, theoretically, expected to be a good predictor of a citizen's choice to obey the police's requests for compliance. Muir's (1977) paradox of face indicates that a nasty reputation (which could be established by adopting coercive tactics as an initial approach) can serve as a "shot across the bow" in police-citizen encounters. Social interactionists would argue that more forceful interaction would indicate an imbalance in coercive power and generate a situation where citizens are inclined to comply (Tedeschi and Felson, 1994:168). In contrast to the weight placed on entry tactics, Sykes and Brent (1983) note that the *persistence* of officers in regulating citizen behavior, even without increasing coercive power, typically results in compliance.

A second hypothesis is that a citizen is more likely to comply when the police indicate that action in which they are engaged is an "arrestable" offense. A threat of arrest, which indicates a severe negative social consequence, is likely to increase the stakes of the compliance game for the target. We are arguing, however, for a standard that is linked to a *consequence*. The suggestion that one's behavior is illegal can take many forms from subtle to overt. The more overt includes a linkage with arrest, or arrest as a consequence of future inaction. This more narrow category is the area from which we draw our hypothesis that, in those situations where police indicate that an offense is arrestable, or indicate that arrest could follow noncompliance, a citizen will have a greater stake in bringing his/her behavior in line with the articulated standard. We argue that the consequences that police intimate or threaten are more likely to convey the extent of a citizen's stake than an abstract statute.[2] That is, they convey the seriousness of the police's intent to make this event more costly in terms of liberty, if cooperation is not forthcoming.

The presence of an audience of police or citizens represents an important pair of predictors for social interactionist theory. The likelihood of citizen compliance when subjected to an officer's authority is hypothesized to be inversely related to citizen audience size. Acquiescence in front of a crowd represents a loss of face, and hence a request is more likely to be challenged (Lanza-Kaduce and Greenleaf, 1993; Muir, 1977; Tedeschi and Felson, 1994). The presence of a larger number of citizens and bystanders represents an increased stake in the maintenance of face, assuming they represent a constituency with whom the target identifies.

Interestingly, Paternoster et al. (1997) hypothesize that efforts at exerting control represent violations of procedural justice concerns and could relate to future noncompliance. They propose, therefore, that cases where there is more coercion (in the form of handcuffing) are more likely to result in noncompliance, measured as future offending, than cases where less coercion is used. This offers an alternative conceptualization of what coercive acts mean to the citizen. From this perspective they are seen as unjustifiable intrusions that render the transaction illegitimate. These two hypotheses represent somewhat competing images of citizens' decision calculus, where one conceives of the citizen as an instrumental avoider of pain, the other as a seeker of justice. These images can be reconciled if a denial of justice is considered a "pain," however, the avoidance of negative stimuli would have us predict that greater pain, in the form of coercion, would result in greater future compliance. Paternoster et al.'s (1997) finding indicates that, if indeed coercion stirs a sense of injustice, then a "tipping point" might exist, whereby citizens interpret coercion at lower levels as an appropriate tactic and are swayed to conformance by its use but are stirred to rebellion when it crosses a threshold and is perceived as inappropriate and unwarranted. Again we are limited by not knowing *how* citizens interpret police actions or those characteristics with which this perception varies.

Targets possessing weapons are more likely to be noncompliant since they possess a tool that can empower their resistance, or as stated above, increase their coercive power. The number of officers present at an encounter is also representative of the coercive balance of power. The number of officers should be positively related to the likelihood of a target's compliance. More officers represent a greater threat to the individual and a rational calculator would consider the odds of thwarting the will of several officers as having a low probability of success.

We argue that officer gender is a proxy for targets' perceptions of threat, with male police officers being perceived as a greater threat than female officers. The image that an officer can project at entry is a combination of tactics and *who* the officer is (Manning, 1977). Gender role stereotypes that are held by both the police and citizens are likely to reinforce the perceptions of relative power (Gilligan, 1982:167).

Generally, the effects of gender are most likely to be exhibited as an interaction between target gender and officer gender, where male officers are most dominant over female targets.[3] Officer-suspect dyads that share the same gender are likely on equal footing, in terms of perceptions of gender as a communicator of relative threat. Finally, female officers attempting to gain compliance over male suspects are likely to represent cases where the male citizen has perceptions of superior coercive power within the dyad structure (e.g., Katz, 1988). The effects of gender interactions are likely to be masked by potential systematic differences in tactical choices (Riksheim and Chermak, 1993:309). The examination of micro-level processing, however, allows for the control of many tactical choices, isolating the effect that perceptions of gender may have on the coercive balance of power. More succinctly, the estimation of a model not accounting for tactical choices could confuse gender effects with systematic gender differences in tactical choices. Controlling for tactics that are "procedurally just" and "more or less coercive" allows the unique effect of these gender differences to be more accurately estimated.

THIRD PARTY EFFECTS

Another "stake" in compliance is the existence of a third party that encourages compliance or noncompliance at the scene. A confederate will assist in anchoring a citizen to a position of rebellion or conformance (Milgram, 1973: 116-121). Third parties that promote noncompliance can do so in two ways. First, the third party can openly request that the citizen defy the police request. This represents a blatant stake in *nonconformity* for the compliance target. Second, the third party, as a bystander or participant can be disrespectful of the police, resist their authority, and become noncompliant themselves. This, in effect, provides a behavioral model for the target. The confederate provides behavioral cues with regard to how one handles the police in these situations, and this is likely to have an influence on the target's own decision calculus. In fact, it is conceivable that such behavior by a third party is likely to have more powerful effects on a target than a verbal encouragement, since the third party is putting his or her liberty at risk, and cooperation by the target citizen might jeopardize that liberty. Cooperating third parties, as noted by Mastrofski and colleagues (1996), make the police task easier, inasmuch as they are providing the citizen with "cover" for complying.

Conformance will be perceived as a mechanism to maintain the relationship with the third party and will follow pathways similar to those listed above: third parties who demonstrate respectful and deferential actions, or actions affirming the need for cooperation with police are likely to encourage a target's compliance.

The discussion of third party, as a "stake," departs from researchers' earlier hypotheses regarding such a presence at the police-citizen encounter. The phenomenon was viewed through Black's (1993) theory of the third party, which suggested that the third party adds more weight to the police as a social control mechanism. The current reformulation does not discount that conception of the third party, it merely puts in the argot of social interactionist theory. The mechanism through which the third party functions is considered to be one of identification. A citizen is "controlled" or "encouraged to rebel" by his or her identification with the third party. These two conceptions of the third party are eminently compatible, and this reformulation recognizes that the police can both enhance their position through a cooperative third party, or have it undercut by a rebellious third party.

Beyond providing role models, third parties can also affect the outcome of the compliance game through their relationship to the target. The presence of an adversary, for example, clearly transforms the police-citizen encounter into a contest in which police must mediate, take sides, and deliver street-level verdicts. Adversaries are likely to reduce the likelihood of compliance since the target is vying for a favorable outcome, and we can infer that police requests for compliance may be reduced, holding other effects constant, when such competition for outcomes is present.

Relatives also represent a third party, albeit one that has a "handle" on the target citizen. The presence of relatives, by themselves, however, does not clarify what one would predict about the likelihood of compliance. Hence one must consider the valence of relatives as a presence at the scene. If the target is in conflict with a relative at the scene, we argue that the negative "adversary" effect noted above will be enhanced (Mastrofski and colleagues, 1996) and the likelihood of target compliance will decrease. Conversely, a relative that is present but not in an adversarial role represents a controlling effect, like the restraining impact of a social bond (Hirschi, 1969). A non-adversarial relative presence is, we argue, a force moving citizens towards conformity in general and compliance in the specific police-citizen encounter.

CITIZEN CHARACTERISTICS

Thus far we have discussed the utility of coercion at gaining compliance and the importance of the initial self-presentation of parties in shaping future interaction. At several points we have noted caveats on simplifying assumptions we make about how police actions are interpreted by citizen-targets. In this section we will explore factors that arguably condition interpretation of police actions, and present theoretical justifications for their presence in a model of citizen compliance.

Three other citizen characteristics are also hypothesized to have an impact on the likelihood of compliance. The first, youthfulness, is associated with a proclivity for nonconforming behavior. The age-crime relationship indicates that youthful citizens are less cemented into societal structures when compared with their older counterparts. We would hypothesize that youths would therefore be more likely to rebel against a source of authority, such as a police request for compliance. Research indicates that youths hold stronger attitudes of legal cynicism and are typically less satisfied with police (Sampson and Bartusch, 1998). Hence, we argue that observed behavior is a product of these unmeasured attitudes.

Citizen race provides contradictory hypotheses regarding the likelihood of conforming. One could argue that citizens in the majority perceive themselves as being more powerful in relation to the authority of the police, and would therefore perceive fewer imbalances when rebelling against a police demand for compliance. Conversely, one could argue that minority citizens accord less deference to the hegemonic order than those in the majority; therefore they would be less compelled, on balance, to conform to a standard demanded by police. Hagan and Albonetti (1982) found a relationship between minority status and negative perceptions of the police and police actions. It is also conceivable that race conditions one's interpretation of authority actions and could result in differential response to the same stimuli (Erez, 1984; Kerner, 1968: 299-307; Dunham and Alpert, 1988). Both perspectives seem equally plausible, but leave us without a firm prediction for the direction of minority status's effect.

The third citizen characteristic that could be relevant to understanding the dynamics of citizen compliance is social class. Luckenbill and Doyle (1989) argue that lower class citizens are more likely to be "disputatious" in dealing with personal interactions. This theory indicates that, holding all else constant, lower class citizens should be more likely to resist the authority of police compared with those citizens who are in the middle or upper classes. If social class is a predictor of disputatious attitudes, then we would expect that those attitudes would condition the citizen's interpretation of officer actions and lead to lower levels of conformance. Differences in the individual's evaluation of the police might be systematically linked to one's position in the class structure (Hagan and Albonetti, 1982). An inverse relationship between social class and perceptions of police legitimacy, for instance, would likely lead to lower levels of compliance for lower social class citizens, net of tactics and other characteristics. Both sets of hypothesized intervening attitudes predict that, *ceteris paribus*, citizens with lower socioeconomic status would be less compliant.

OFFICER TRAITS

We argue that an officer characteristic important for understanding citizen compliance is the race of the officer. Citizens may have differential conceptions of authorities based on the authority's race. We argue that the race of the officer contributes to the perceived legitimacy of his or her actions. Officers that represent the dominant culture may be seen as more authoritative than minority officers (Mastrofski and colleagues, 1996). It is also plausible that citizens are more responsive to authorities that share their characteristics (in essence an interaction effect between race of citizens and race of officers). These two hypotheses produce conflicting predictions. The former would suggest that white officers would be more successful in gaining conformance due to their identification with the hegemonic power structures. The latter suggests that, same race dyads would produce greater levels of citizen conformity. Regardless of the direction of predictions, it is clear that officer race should play an important role in predicting citizen responses to requests for compliance.

CITIZEN IRRATIONALITY

The theories that have been drawn upon thus far have assumed that the citizen *qua* target of compliance is a rational calculator, and is able to perceive costs, benefits, justice, and fairness in the procedures used by the authorities. This rationality does not require an omniscient calculus of costs and benefits or fairness and justice, but should approximate a probabilistic assessment of a rational calculator. The hypotheses that have been presented in the preceding pages rely upon the citizen to interpret the actions of the police officer and use them as aids in deciding to comply or rebel.

Citizens are not perfectly rational, nor are they wholly irrational (for the sake of argument); however, greater amounts of citizen irrationality should predict noncompliance. A citizen who cannot accurately calculate benefits and costs is unlikely to weigh consequences of action and becomes an object that is difficult for police to handle in a routine fashion. The "crazy-brave," for example, represents citizens whose calculus has been harmed by their diminution of mental capacity (Muir, 1977).

We identify the affects of alcohol and other drugs, strong emotion, and apparent mental illness as indicia of lowered rationality. Diminished rationality is likely to be negatively related to compliance. The impaired citizen is less able to use social cues to make judgments, and the literature indicates that they are more likely to misinterpret their own coercive power in such situations (Tedeschi and Felson, 1994).

Alcohol and other drugs affect the perceptions of users and are known to impair judgment and response times.

"Imbibing alcohol can facilitate coercive actions. A person who has been drinking may become less attentive to social cues and may make more hostile attributions of intention. Drinking may also cause a narrowing of perception to immediate cues with disattention to remote events or abstract principles....[Alcohol's] effects reduce the perception of costs and, hence, increase the likelihood that coercive actions that are antinormative or viewed negatively by an audience will be performed." (Tedeschi and Felson, 1994: 199-200).

Alcohol use is associated with disinhibition, impairment of judgment, and the enhancement of aggression. This leads to the hypothesis that the citizen under the influence of alcohol will be more resistant to officer actions and tactics. We might also expect that the inebriated citizen is likely to be more aggressive against the officer that could lead to a quick abandonment of compliance tactics for more legal strategies. In essence, alcohol appears to appeal to our worst angels. It undermines individuals' ability to rationally calculate the costs and consequences of actions. Furthermore, it is associated with elevated levels of aggression (Mongrain and Standing, 1989; Steele and Southwick, 1985). The presence of strong emotion is another factor that, we argue, undermines the rational calculation of costs and benefits. Citizens in the grip of emotion are, by definition, less rational than their calm counterparts. Emotion's effect on behavior is documented by Scheff and Retzigner (1991) and Zillmann (1979; 1983).

"Zillman (1979, 1983) proposed that three factors are important for explaining aggressive behavior: (a) the evocation of excitation or arousal associated with emotional states, (b) the dispositions or learned behavior patterns of the individual, and c) the monitoring function of higher cognitive processes that appraise the appropriateness of both emotional states and courses of behavior. Endangerment of the person's well-being produces a temporary increase in sympathetic arousal. Endangerment is defined in terms of pain, discomfort, and debasement -- all of which produce an emergency reaction in the form of physiological arousal and learned behaviors." (Tedeschi and Felson, 1994: 75).

Anger, which is associated with coercion and violence, also affects perceptions and actions. Indicators of anger are not necessarily openly displayed by a party (Tedeschi and Felson, 1994).

"Anger arousal disrupts and disorganizes cognitive processes. A tendency of angry people is to simplify information processing and to make judgements that are more black and white than in calmer circumstances (R.K. White, 1968). Arousal affects the speed of information processing and reduces attentional capacity (Masters, Felleman, and Barden, 1981; Meichenbaum and Gilmore, 1984). Complex behaviors are disrupted. The verbal behavior of an angry person may become disorganized, and it may become more difficult for them to clearly express a grievance. It is cognitively easier to verbally abuse the other person than it is to present a well-organized and persuasive communication about the legitimacy of one's complaint. Deleterious effects of anger arousal on cognitive processes may cause reactions to become more crude and impulsive. Thus the admonition to count to 10 when angry (cf. Tavris, 1982)." (Tedeschi and Felson, 1994: 234-235).

Research by psychologists indicates that anger and strong emotion function in a way similar to alcohol and other drugs. Anger tends to reduce the processing capacity that we identify as necessary for rational calculation. Furthermore, it appears that strong emotion may distort perceptions and enhance the motivation to be aggressive. These factors lead us to conclude that, ceteris paribus, those individuals who are in the grip of strong emotions are less likely to comply with police requests to cease misbehavior.

The presence of apparent mental illness in citizens with whom the police interact presents an especially difficult situation similar to those where a citizen is influenced by alcohol or strong emotions. The presence of a mental illness, by definition, indicates that the citizen is operating with a diminished rational-intellectual capacity.[4] In such cases it is hypothesized that citizens are likely to be less inclined to comply with the police. This could be due to an inability to interpret the cues officers introduce, a diminished ability to assess the consequences of actions, or a heightened impulsivity that will generate more aggressive behavior.

OTHER THEORETICAL CONSIDERATIONS

Thus far we have opted to describe citizens using a social interactionist framework for understanding their perceptions, calculations, and reactions to stimuli. This is not the only theory that might be useful in understanding why citizens obey. In the following sections we will argue that procedural justice concerns and context are vital to understanding compliance in police-citizen encounters. It is necessary, however, to first address two theoretical domains, conflict theory and police wisdom, adopted in the previous studies of compliance done by Mastrofski and colleagues (1996) and McCluskey et al. (1999).

A central critique of conflict theory as an explanation of citizen compliance with police requests is that it lacks a component of agency.[5] The linkage between class and outcome is mediated by an unexplained mechanism. Lanza-Kaduce and Greenleaf (1994) delineate a comprehensive set of hypotheses rooted in the conflict tradition, but fail to suggest what causal mechanism links citizen rebellion against authority to their class position.   Turk's (1969:30-78) discourse on norm resistance, from which the aforementioned hypotheses are derived, is focused on the relative positions of authorities and subjects *vis a vis* a larger culture.   These ideas draw us outside the unique sequencing of events during individual interaction and look more towards the relative position of the actors in social space.   Black's (1995) theorizing on the sociology of law offers a similar framework. In our estimation it addresses the issue of police-citizen interaction at a similar level, and assumes that interpersonal actions are relatively homogenous when social space is controlled, or individual actions are largely irrelevant in predicting outcomes.   The primary assumption that we have adopted herein is that the interaction of police and citizens is heterogeneous.   Police use different approaches, different levels of authority, and citizen's responses are also individualized.   From such an assumption we argue that race, youthfulness, or gender are relevant, but that the causal mechanisms through which differences along these social dimensions are manifested operate at a microsocial level.   For example, it is conceivable that police tactics and citizen responses vary by gender and ethnicity.   There is no reason why conflict theorists and social interactionists need to be in competition, rather the two are complementary.   In the current analysis, however, the microsocial processes will be emphasized over the structural effects which one's social characteristics may manifest.

The exclusion of "police wisdom" represents a similar concern for developing a comprehensive explanation that is rooted in theory. Police wisdom, in many instances, is coterminous with social theory and where that is true it will be included in the model.   For example, intoxicated or otherwise disturbed citizens are considered to present especially difficult cases to the officer in the police literature (Muir, 1977; Mastrofski and colleagues, 1996).   While a valuable nugget of police wisdom, this concept also has roots in the theoretical tradition of social interactionism compiled by Tedeschi and Felson (1994).   The objective of this research is to examine the general nature of human interaction through the specific case of police-citizen encounters; therefore we argue that more general principles, applicable across human settings, ought to be adopted as an explanatory framework.

CHAPTER TWO

PROCEDURAL JUSTICE AND COMPLIANCE

Issues of fairness and justice and their meanings for individuals are ancient ones (Plato, 360 B.C./1992). Social philosophers have examined fairness and justice in the context of exchange theory (Blau, 1964; Homans, 1961) and in terms of distributive justice (Rawls, 1971). These are rooted in the equity of outcomes or allocations (Leventhal, 1980). Thibaut and Walker (1975) redefined "justice" and "fairness" into two components that included the original notion of distributive justice that Rawls (1971) explored and a second component identified as procedural justice. The idea of procedural justice is what we draw upon for hypotheses concerning compliance in police-citizen encounters.

Procedural justice, as conceived by Thibaut and Walker, is rooted in fair procedures or those procedures which, on balance, are perceived to generate the fairest outcomes for individuals. Individuals, it is argued, favor mechanisms that give them more process control and more decision control. These concepts mirror the ideas of fair processing of disputes and the equity in outcomes which are consistent with an instrumentalist view of human behavior. Early research on procedural justice focused on dispute resolution and compared various forms of adversary process with the satisfaction of disputants in mock trials. Distributive and procedural components were identified in research on perceptions of justice and fairness, and subsequent research continued to refine the meaning of procedural justice. The key in discriminating between distributive justice and procedural justice is that the former is rooted in instrumental concerns and the latter is rooted in normative concern (Leventhal, 1980; Paternoster et al., 1997). Instrumental concerns of distributive justice are represented by equitable distribution of tangible benefits to an actor. Normative concerns of procedural justice are represented by ideals such as fairness and justice independent of the instrumental outcomes. It is important to note that this early research was concerned with issues of *perception* and *perceived satisfaction*, not *behaviors* such as compliance with an authority's requests.

Leventhal (1980) elaborated on Thibaut and Walker's ideas of procedural justice. He argued that qualities of "fair procedures" could be identified *a priori* and offered six hypotheses on perceptions of procedural fairness. These included consistency in decision making, the suppression of bias in decision making, accuracy of the decision, whether the decision is correctable, whether the individual is afforded an opportunity for representation, and whether the procedures comport with the moral and ethical values of the individual (Leventhal, 1980: 41-46).

Research on procedural justice continued to examine the psychological dimensions of fairness and its effect on the behavior of citizens involved in various administrative and legal proceedings. McEwen and Maiman (1984) examined the effect of fair procedures on citizens' decisions to comply with small claims court settlements, and found that mediation was more successful than adversarial procedures in generating compliant outcomes, even after controlling for the favorability of the outcome. In the authors' opinion, that finding was rooted in the fact that mediation encouraged participation, consent, and perceptions of fairness. Hence, perceptions of procedural justice (i.e., "I am being treated fairly") were connected to compliant behavior in this setting.

Tyler's (1988) exploration of procedural justice integrated the work of Thibaut and Walker and Leventhal. This research, using a panel of citizens from Chicago, explored satisfaction and perceptions of contacts with courts and police. Tyler found overall support for the importance of "fair procedures" in shaping citizens' perceptions net of favorability of outcomes. This research also buttresses the notion that distributive justice and procedural justice, though related, are distinct phenomena, since favorability of outcomes had a separate impact on perceptions.

Tyler also used his initial analysis in order to explore the meaning of procedural justice among individuals. In essence, this amounted to testing whether the constructs specified by Leventhal were an adequate enumeration of cognitive dimensions of procedural justice:

"The results of the regression analysis suggest that the criteria of procedural justice assessed explain most of the variance in citizen judgments about whether fair procedures were used (69 percent). Seven aspects of procedural justice make an independent contribution to assessments of process fairness: the effort of the authorities to be fair; their honesty; whether their behavior is consistent with ethical standards; whether opportunities for representation are given; the quality of the decisions made; whether opportunities to appeal decisions exist; and whether the behavior of the authorities shows bias" (1988:21).

Tyler's research generated several specific hypotheses regarding citizens' perceptions of fair procedures: The opportunity for representation, impartiality of the authorities, the quality of the decision (i.e. the effort used to make a decision), and the ethicality of the authorities were important and positive predictors of perceived fairness. The relative importance of predictors of the perceptions of procedural justice varied by setting. For example, in situations where disputes were occurring, representation and impartiality were given more weight in shaping perceptions of fairness.

A general model of procedural fairness can be specified if one adopts Tyler's (1988) elaboration and integration of the work done by Thibaut and Walker (1975) and Leventhal (1980). Lind and Tyler's (1988) further exploration of the contours of procedural justice extended the model to include compliant behavior as an outcome. As noted above, the initial research on procedural justice was largely restricted to psychological constructs, perceptions, and attitudes towards various authorities. This work extended the model from a mental/psychological phenomenon (perceptions of fairness predicted by perceptions of authority actions), to a model that included the prediction of behavioral outcomes based on individuals' interpretations of the fairness of an authority's actions. In terms of procedures that increase compliance, the authors conclude those that are successful allow voice for the individual, are ethically sound, and are fair and impartial. Furthermore, the procedural justice effects are ubiquitous, that is they are present in all social settings. Irrespective of outcomes that an individual obtains, as perceived procedural justice increases, the likelihood of compliance increases as well (1988: Ch. 9&10). It is important to note that while procedures exercise a strong effect on satisfaction (a belief) they exert only a modest impact in predicting compliant *behavior* (Lind and Tyler, 1988).

Examining compliance in police-citizen contexts through the lens of procedural justice requires an exploration of previous research involving those situations. Data from the Richmond study (Mastrofski and colleagues, 1996) and the Project on Policing Neighborhoods (McCluskey et al., 1999) indicate, for example, that disrespectful officer behavior reduces the likelihood of citizen compliance. Other tactical variation embedded within encounters represents micro-processual interactions between the police and the compliance target. Further elaboration of the model, with ideas developed from procedural justice literature, will enhance our understanding of what *actions* affect citizen compliance.

PROCESSING AND PROCEDURAL JUSTICE

As noted above, research on procedural justice has largely emanated from the study of the adjudicatory process (McEwen and Maiman, 1984; Tyler, 1988). Lind and Tyler (1988) have noted that the effects of procedural justice can be observed in diverse settings, including police-citizen encounters. This research has focused on psychological and behavioral responses of citizens to authorities, or more precisely the satisfaction with contacts and the compliance with authorities (Paternoster et al., 1997; Tyler, 1990; Tyler and Folger, 1980). The police-citizen encounter in which a police officer requests compliance is most likely to present a dynamic similar to an adjudicatory hearing. The compliance request represents, to some extent, the instantaneous judgment of the officer as an agent of the state. The events with which we are dealing are similar to those present in the corresponding research involving the adjudicatory process, but herein decisions are made with less deliberation and once made, these decisions reflect the taking of a side in a dispute.

Linkages between psychological assessments of procedural fairness, generally, and an individual's decision to comply is based upon a large body of research (Lind and Tyler, 1988; Tyler, 1997). Regrettably, there is limited information on the precise actions of authorities that generate perceptions of procedural fairness. The research indicates that there is a linkage between authority action (of some unspecified nature), the citizen's perception of fairness, and the citizen's decision to comply.

The research described above models the effects of perceptions on decisions to comply. When the unmeasured component of authority action is viewed as being fair, this increases the legitimacy of the authority's ability to impose a decision, and in turn leads to an increased likelihood of compliance. As legitimacy increases then obedience to requests is more likely to be forthcoming from a target (Milgram, 1973: 97). Although research has demonstrated little about the *specific* actions which produce fairness perceptions, it does, however, allow us to identify actions and tactics that comport with the perceptions they hypothetically generate. Certainly, we cannot haphazardly draw a direct causal arrow from any authority action to the decision to comply. Choosing appropriate actions requires that we acknowledge the subjective interpretation by the individual citizen (Lind and Tyler, 1988; Paternoster et al., 1997). Hypotheses are developed below that conservatively mirror the literature in social psychology that has attempted to model psychological constructs, and attempts to identify the authority behavior that is the plausible antecedent of procedural justice attitudes.

An ideal model of procedural justice effects would consist of the actions of authorities, the interpretations of individuals, and the outcome decision. We could then examine how authorities' actions condition perceptions of procedural justice and produce compliant or noncompliant outcomes. Presently, there is little opportunity to make such linkages outside of the laboratory (Thibaut and Walker, 1975; Lind and Tyler, 1988). Nonetheless we can specify objective actions that should produce, on balance, the desiderata of procedural justice. For heuristic purposes we will trace the entire three stage model out, while admitting that the "black box" of subjective citizen interpretation of procedural justice as a legitimating factor will be outside the boundaries of empirical analysis in this inquiry.

An examination of perceived procedural justice's impact on citizen cooperation and compliance requires a more precise conceptualization and measurement than has been undertaken to date. For example, existing research (Mastrofski and colleagues, 1996 and Wiley and Hudik, 1974), indicates that disrespectful action or inaction by police will provoke noncompliance. We argue that measures of disrespect represent, albeit incompletely, Leventhal's concept of *ethicality* (see also Tyler, 1988). Hence, the presence of disrespectful officer behavior will likely generate less compliance. This hypothesis connects an officer action (disrespect), with an interpretive value judgment by the citizen (perception) and ultimately leads to the generation of noncompliant behavior.[1]

Conversely, respectful treatment, previously measured by researchers examining police-citizen interactions as partially or completely fulfilling citizen's requests or comforting them, is also a component of procedural justice. Respectful treatment is hypothesized to generate compliance through ethicality's generation of a sense of "fairness." Officers who obey citizen desires and treat them with respect are more likely to get compliance when it is requested. Tyler and Kerstetter (1994) note that policing, especially community policing which relies on personal authority, requires that police be seen as benevolent and fair to gain the consent of those whom they police.[2] Respectful treatment is one such tactical indicator of benevolence and procedural fairness. Such behavior by authorities, in theory, reinforces the perceived self-worth of compliance targets and reinvests them in the larger social milieu (Lane, 1988; Tyler, 1997).

The second component of procedural justice theory that we can link with an authority's behavior is the idea of representation or voice. If an officer accepts information, and indicates that he/she is listening to the individual, this would represent an opportunity for the citizen to express himself or herself. Theory and research indicate that citizens who are afforded such opportunity are more likely to be satisfied and compliant (Tyler, 1990; Tyler, 1998; Tyler, 2001; Tyler, Rasinski, and Spodick, 1985). Accepting the input of a compliance target should, in theory, generate a sense of unbiasedness and impartiality, and reinforce the citizen's belief that they are getting a voice. Such an opportunity to present one's story to an authority is likely to increase the sense of fairness and legitimacy (Hudson, 1970), and ceteris paribus, the likelihood of achieving citizen compliance.

Conversely, in the dynamic of police-citizen relations, an officer can "cut off" communication with a citizen, whereby they terminate the discussion with a compliance target without allowing a complete airing of the target's position. Situations where compliance targets are denied voice, by ignoring, actively silencing, or commanding silence, are more likely to be perceived as a denial of due consideration. Leventhal (1980), Tyler (1988), and Lind and Tyler (1988) indicate that such an act would be perceived as "unfair" and would generate, ceteris paribus, target noncompliance with authorities' requests. From the viewpoint of a citizen this phenomenon is partially a *negation of voice*, partially an example of a violation of the norms of *ethicality* (denial of conduct norms of listening to a party); an indication that the authorities are not interested in gaining full information to make a *quality decision*, and partially an indicator of *decision maker bias*. Regardless of how the perceptual component of "fair procedures" is generated (i.e., it could have an effect on several perceived dimensions), it is plausible to hypothesize that termination of voice will reduce compliance.

Another objective police action, which is plausibly interpreted as an indicator of fair procedures, is the police's self-directed search for information. Police officers that actively seek the input of citizens are more likely to engender a perception of fairness from a compliance target. This search for information should, in theory, generate a sense that the officer is attempting to make a quality decision and allowing for individual representation through the self-directed gathering of information (this tactic goes beyond the proffer of a story, herein the target is asked by police to contribute factual information and interpret the events). Such an opportunity to present one's story, or an interpretation of the events *at the behest of an authority* (the authority's request for information is what distinguishes this from the previously mentioned voice effects) should increase perceived fairness and legitimacy, and ceteris paribus, the likelihood of achieving citizen compliance.

Impartiality is an important determinant of fairness and the establishment of legitimacy. To the extent that an officer "takes a side," or in the Blackian (1993) sense becomes more partisan, the less likely citizens are to perceive the procedure as fair. Partisanship would be present in those cases where police adopt the position of another person present, and use that as a rationale for resolving the situation. When police appeal to a standard clearly derived from a disputant ("Mary wants you to leave for the night") and not from their own judgment and evaluation ("I think you ought to leave for the night") the police will be perceived as partisan. In those events where partisanship or bias is detected, it is argued that perceptions of fairness will, on balance, decrease, regardless of the party that is favored. Interests in distributive justice might make favorable partisanship acceptable, but in the procedural sense, regardless of the target of partisanship, favoritism must be viewed as reducing the perceived fairness of the process. Therefore, it is necessary to establish whether police actively take a partisan position in a dispute, or rather remain an unbiased mediator.

Decisions tinged with bias are less likely to be accorded legitimacy, and those encounters where the police are more partisan in resolving disputes will result in lower levels of compliant behavior among citizens.

Finally, Tyler (1988; 1990) notes the importance of "morality" in determining whether a procedure is deemed legitimate and fair. This concept has limited applicability in the context of police-citizen interactions where the attitudinal valences of citizens are unknown. Citizen behavior, however, like police behavior, may reflect the perception of "morality" of police intervention and authority. Those situations where citizens make positive statements about police presence ("Glad you are here," or "Thanks for responding") indicate instances where they believe the police presence to be morally justifiable. We would suggest that those situations (again absent attitudinal valences) that are marked by verbalizations that reject the police's presence are important indicators of citizen's perceptions of the morality and legitimacy of police intervention. Examples would include instances where citizens question their presence, make demeaning remarks regarding their presence, or otherwise verbalize that they are "not needed" to intervene.

These negative verbalizations should be clearly demarcated from those indicating noncompliance and rebellion. Acts of disrespect aside from noncompliance would be included among examples of citizens who deny the moral legitimacy of police authority through instrumental or expressive behavior. Regardless, citizens who withdraw legitimacy from the police's presence are less likely to comply and those who grant moral legitimacy to police presence should be inclined to acquiesce to police requests for compliance (Tyler, 1997). There are two problems with capturing a citizen's sense of police legitimacy. First, the social interactionist position outlined above is posited on actors reacting to stimuli. Adopting target actions to predict other actions of the same target creates a problem with respect to a police action that might be the cause of both behaviors. To correct for the possibility of mutual causation, the citizen's morality must precede *any* police action (verbal or physical) that might elicit a response from the target. Essentially we are arguing for the coding of a citizen "entry" tactic that sheds light on this attitudinal valence. The second problem with this scheme is that it neglects to account for attitudes of participants and relies on congruity between their overt actions and the actual attitudes that they possess. The linkage between attitudes and behavior has limited support (Azjen, 1987) and is likely to contribute to measurement error in a construct limited only to overt citizen behaviors.

One overarching indicator of procedural legitimacy is the presence of probable cause for arrest with regard to the target citizen. In those instances where police operate under probable cause they have a de facto legitimacy to make demands upon the citizen. Conversely, in those cases where probable cause is absent police lack such a reservoir of legitimacy. We thus propose that instances where police have probable cause, and make compliance requests, citizens will be more apt to acquiesce than when probable cause is not present.

The proposed relationships are arguably the best set of objective police and citizen actions that comport with the various hypothesized relationships between procedural justice and compliance found in the literature on the social psychology of justice (Leventhal, 1980; Tyler, 1988; Lind and Tyler, 1988; Thibaut and Walker, 1975; Tyler, 1990; and Tyler, 1997). The more direct model that we are testing forgoes the transformation of an authority's action into a calculus of procedural justice, reinforcing legitimacy, and ultimately impacting citizen behavior. Instead it captures the behaviors of police and citizens and uses the objective content to specify a relationship with a citizen's decision to comply. We are unable to include, and leave unmeasured, the extent to which citizens evaluate the nature of police actions with the exception of the aforementioned indicators of morality. For policy makers the relationship between tactic and outcome largely ignores the cognitive transformation of behavioral signals when a behavioral outcome is being measured. Regardless of the theoretical underpinnings, we are ultimately interested in exploring whether the specified tactics affect citizens' decisions to comply. Nonetheless the rooting of these measures in existing theory provides a stronger argument for their inclusion in a model of citizen compliance. Other research using different methods could test the relationships between authorities' actions and targets' attitudes and perceptions.

Overall, we have attempted to conceptualize police actions that are congruent with the perceptions measured in a large body of procedural justice research. The actions are loosely tied to the labels offered by Leventhal (1980) and others, but represent factors to which citizens are likely to attend in a police-citizen encounter. In no way can this research explicitly link, for instance, information seeking behaviors with the sense of decision-making quality or representation. Hence, the labels that we adopt are somewhat arbitrary if they describe a "sense of justice'" and not a precise police action such as displays of disrespect.

CONTEXTUAL EFFECTS ON COMPLIANCE OUTCOMES

The hypotheses offered thus far for predicting compliance outcomes are rooted in the micro-level processes of the police-citizen encounter. Justice and fairness, coercion, citizen perceptions and irrationality are hypothesized to affect the probability of police attaining compliance. Below we argue that an important overlay on this micro-processual perspective is the context in which an encounter occurs.

We first examine a heretofore unmentioned context, that of the location of the encounter, and its level of concentrated disadvantage. Then we turn our attention briefly to three elements that may condition how citizens behave in the face of various stimuli. These include whether there is an adversary present, whether the person is under the influence of any irrational elements, and whether there is probable cause to arrest the target.

Place as Context

Social theorists including Durkheim (1893) have argued that social groups have differing levels of attachment or bonding to the larger society. For Durkheim this was captured in the concepts *collective conscience,* social solidarity, and alienation. This suggests that forces external to the individual keep him or her "cemented" in the larger social composite. An individual will become anomic when the bonds are weakened. This anomie allows the individual to engage in deviant behavior.

The classic statement of macro-level social control theory in criminology was made by Shaw and McKay (1942) and has been characterized by Kornhauser as social control theory at the macro-level (1978). The factors that have been identified as vital components of aggregate social control include racial heterogeneity, mobility of citizens, and the amount of poverty present in an ecological area or neighborhood (e.g., Shaw and McKay, 1942; Warner and Pierce, 1992). The rebirth of contextual analysis has led to a renewed interest in the effects that macro-level variables can have on criminal justice decision-making (Klinger, 1997; Warner, 1997). The research done on decision-making has been rooted in the theories of Shaw and McKay (e.g.,

Smith, 1986). If research uncovers macro level effects on police officers' decision making or report taking (Smith 1986; Warner, 1997), then research on citizens' decisions, arguably the target intended by the theorists, should consider whether contextual effects impact citizens' decision patterns.[3]

We argue that citizen compliance with requests to cease misbehavior and for self-control is an important decision point for the citizen in this social interaction and that it is likely to be affected by the ecological context within which that activity occurs. The large body of social control theory provides a reference point for predicting outcomes and suggests that the informal controls that are present or absent across ecological contexts may influence the citizen's decisions (Goldstein, 1994).[4]

The context of social interactions has been largely overlooked by previous examinations of citizen compliance with police requests (e.g., Mastrofski and colleagues, 1996 and McCluskey and Mastrofski, 1997), with the exception of determining whether the event took place in a public or private setting. Nevertheless, literature spanning criminological theories and the administration of criminal justice provides a framework for the inclusion of contextual variables in a model of compliance. To develop a hypothesis regarding the effects of encounter context on citizen behavior we first must elaborate on noncompliance and its relationship to deviance. Nonconformance to a request by an authority is justifiable in cases of oppression and in cases where the authority is illegitimate. In the cases of police-citizen contacts we assume that police are acting within their legitimate social mandate to impose a solution on the situation at hand. The commands or requests that they are issuing are assumed, in an objective sense, to be neither oppressive nor illegal. Failing to obey the request of the authority represents a breach of "normal" behavior and is, therefore, considered deviant. In summary, our hypothesis is developed with the notion that acquiescence to police authority is a "normal" reaction and that rebellion is a "deviant" reaction.

We argue that conforming or compliant citizen conduct is likely to arise in those encounters where the police are in areas that have more informal social control, once the micro-level predictors have been controlled. This illustrates the need to operationalize informal social control at the macro-level. Theorizing on the behavior of individuals indicates that, with respect to deviance, micro-social and macro-social factors exercise independent effects. Criminological theories are rich with respect to context as Shaw and McKay introduced macro level effects of *mobility, heterogeneity,* and *social class* on individual levels of deviant behavior. Likewise, Cloward and Ohlin (1960) have attempted to explain deviant behavior through structural factors and processes. Similarly, structural factors may also play a role in shaping the outcomes of individual police-citizen contacts wherein the officer asks the citizen to cease misbehavior.

The problem with linking ecological factors to individual behaviors is that there must be a mechanism through which that effect must manifest itself (e.g., Sampson and Groves, 1989). We posit four plausible explanations for ecological effects on individual level compliance behavior. Each assumes that social disorganization or social distress (a concept which mirrors disorganization) must affect a more proximal, but unmeasured factor, through which an effect on compliance travels. First, it is possible that those areas that are socially distressed cause higher levels of individual *strain* among residents when compared with areas that are more socially organized. This comports with the opportunity theory advanced by Cloward and Ohlin (1960). Residents of areas with social distress are more likely to "challenge the legitimacy" of norms. As a result we argue that in such areas police are more likely to have their normative authority challenged, in the form of noncompliance, since residents are likely to suffer higher levels of strain.

Second, it is conceivable that social distress promotes different attitudes toward conflict resolution when compared to areas that are less distressed. Markowitz and Tedeschi (1998) argue that lower class citizens are more likely to absorb attitudes that punitive and combative solutions to conflict are acceptable. Anderson's (1999) ethnography on the "code of the streets" indicates that socially disadvantaged areas are likely to adopt a separate value system that emphasizes the maintenance of one's reputation. Hence, we argue that distressed areas, which contain more citizens in lower socio-economic strata, are likely to have higher rates of noncompliance since "disputatiousness" and reputation, according to theorists, are differentially valued in such areas.

Third, one could argue that citizens in different areas have dissimilar conceptions of justified police action which would, in turn, indirectly affect the likelihood of citizen compliance (e.g. Gurr, 1971:26; Kerner, 1968:299-307). This hypothesis assumes that citizens' perceptions of tactics that police use to gain compliance are predicted by the social distress in the area. For example, the searching of a person might be accepted as justifiable in low distress area but seen as an affront in a high distress area. The reverse is also possible, as citizens in the low distress area might be more critical of the services they receive, which illustrates the difficulty of specifying *a priori* hypotheses between disorganization and perceptions of actions. Research by Hagan and Albonetti (1982), for instance, indicates that class position can condition one's perception of actions by criminal justice agents. Ultimately these effects should be apparent in differing likelihood of compliance between neighborhoods if the tactics of police are controlled, as we argue that tactics that are deemed unfair are more likely to promote rebellion. If an interaction between neighborhood disorganization and perceptions of tactics exists we would expect to find a direct effect of neighborhood disorganization on the likelihood of compliance.

Fourth, the theory of social control indicates that individuals have differential social bonding to the larger society through factors such as attachment (Hirschi, 1969).[5] Socially disorganized areas are likely to be deficient in social networks that Krohn (1986) describes as weaving individuals into the fabric of society. Durkheim's observation that, "we are moral beings to the extent that we are social beings," (1961:64; see also Hirschi, 1969: 18) reinforces the notion that social bonds attach us to a normative societal structure. Recent theoretical and empirical work by Morenoff, Sampson, and Raudenbush (2002) argues that collective efficacy is the intervening mechanism for maintaining neighborhood cohesion. Since noncompliance is a form of misbehavior, weakened attachments, which are arguably greater in disorganized areas, should lead to higher levels of noncompliance, when tactics and other factors are held constant.

These four mechanisms represent a constellation of plausible factors that intervene between social disorganization and individual decisions to comply with police requests to cease misbehavior. Though there are four enumerated, three share the prediction that areas with higher levels of disorganization are likely to have lower levels of compliance, regardless of the mechanism in operation. The fourth, involving differential interpretations of police action, does not clearly specify a direction of the effect. There is strong reason to hypothesize that, holding constant the interactions between police and citizens, the level of social disorganization will negatively impact the likelihood of citizen compliance, despite the lack of clarity regarding the intervening mechanism.

Other "Contexts" of Compliance

Besides the geographic location of the encounter, we argue that several other factors are important and may condition the citizen's response to various stimuli presented by the police. Below we introduce each factor, and suggest how it would likely affect the power of various "procedurally just or unjust" police actions in explaining compliance.

The presence of an adversary transforms the encounter between police and citizen into a much more traditional quasi-judicial proceeding. The importance of evidence presentation in those settings may be an enhanced predictor of compliance, if our theorizing about the importance of fair procedures holds. We would hypothesize that with respect to predicting compliance, the presence of an adversary will enhance the importance of procedural justice concerns, since there are two parties competing for an outcome.

If a citizen is acting under any element of irrationality, we would expect that the explanatory power of the model of compliance to be diminished overall. More explicitly, we would argue that irrationality should reduce the effect of procedurally just actions in predicting compliance outcomes when compared with "rational" citizens. As mentioned previously the elements of irrationality reduce decision-making capacity. Citizens operating under the effects of irrationality, therefore, are less likely to be predictable in the statistical sense.

Finally, we argue that probable cause, as an overarching "legitimating" factor will condition how citizens interpret other police actions during the police-citizen encounter. In cases where probable cause is present citizens are likely to be more attentive to how they are processed and, ceteris paribus, be more likely to base decisions on the "justness" of police action. The reverse is likely to be true for their counterparts who are asked for compliance without the presence of probable cause. Such targets are likely to accord less weight to the "justness" of police actions.

CONCLUSION

In this chapter we have outlined a theory of how police action affects citizen decision making with respect to fairness and justice. The formulation of these hypotheses is built upon the work of Tyler (1990) and Lind and Tyler's (1988) research on procedural justice. We have linked those actions to the likelihood of compliance with police requests.

In addition, we have specified four "contexts" which will interact with models of compliance. From the social ecology tradition we have adopted concentrated disadvantage as a potential conditioning factor. From our own theory we have identified three other factors, the presence of irrationality, presence of an adversary, and the presence of probable cause as elements which may interact with other stimuli in police-citizen encounters.

CHAPTER THREE

CONCEPTUALIZING AND MEASURING COMPLIANCE

THE NATURE OF POLICE-CITIZEN INTERACTION

Two studies have examined citizen compliance with police requests to date and both have been "encounter" based (Mastrofski and colleagues, 1996; McCluskey et al., 1999). That research has treated the police-citizen encounter as a behavioral cross-section, and has largely ignored the micro-social interplay of the authorities and their target. The study of the consequences of human interaction relies on measuring subtle cues, information exchange, and the request-response nature of human communication (Sykes and Brent, 1983). This research addresses the issue of interaction in the course of these encounters and its effect on citizens' decisions to comply, at a level of analysis different from prior efforts.

Prior research on police-citizen encounters is captured at the cross-sectional level. For example, research on police decision-making explores the "causes" of arrest at the encounter level (Smith and Visher, 1981; Ericson, 1981; Mastrofski, Worden, and Snipes, 1995; Novak et al., 2002). The aggregation of human interaction into encounters is akin to a "snapshot" of an event. Such a snapshot is likely to distort the importance of some factors and ignore others altogether. Arguments favoring longitudinal research over cross sectional analysis, as a tool for understanding human development, rest on the same rationale. A snapshot of an event or an individual in time is better for examining structural effects and not the dynamic processes at work in producing social outcomes (e.g., Emerson, 1983; Menard and Elliott, 1994).

Two studies of policing have attempted to capture the police-citizen encounter in a dynamic fashion. Sykes and Brent (1983) describe complex data collection protocols utilized in Midwest City to capture *utterances*. These data allow for the comparison of police-citizen verbal communication in the form of exchanges. Thus, one is able to look at the complex phenomenon of human interaction at its most basic verbal component. Such coding is an onerous task, and the complexity of the data is itself a hurdle that has limited analyses to officers' engagement with a single citizen (Sykes and Brent, 1983). Nevertheless, with respect to capturing the dynamics of social interaction, this research is clearly at the zenith of describing the verbal regulation and interaction between police and citizen.

A second study, Bayley and Bittner's (1984) research on the Denver, Colorado police, represents a less onerous (when compared with the *utterance* level) framework for understanding police-citizen interactions. Bayley (1986) examined the tactical choices that the police make regarding disturbances and traffic stops. The actions of officers were subdivided into the stages of entry/contact, processing, and exit. This distinction gives the research a dynamic sense of how officers conduct themselves in situations and delineates tactics that they adopt at each stage. Tactical choices were found to affect both subsequent tactics and the outcome of the encounters (both outcomes and tactics are largely determined by the police, citizen behaviors were not the primary focus of this work), lending credence to the notion that examinations of police-citizen interaction can benefit from a more precise ordering of events than an encounter level snapshot.

In examining the two methods as mechanisms for creating a template for what police and citizens do in an encounter, it appears that Bayley's proposal of entry, processing, and exit offers a less complete picture than one that captures individual *utterances*. But to understand how police and citizens *interact*, it may be unnecessary to examine every utterance. Instead, one needs to develop two information tracks: First, through formulation of theory, the researcher must be able to produce an *a priori* enumeration of officer and citizen behaviors most likely to affect the specified outcome. Second, the researcher must be able to place events in temporal order. For example, there is strong reason to believe that disrespectful actions by the police would lead to a higher likelihood of noncompliance by targets. Encounters including disrespect by the police, however, vary greatly in terms of the timing of such acts. If an officer continuously asks a citizen to comply and disrespects the citizen as an exit tactic ("You asshole, I wish you would comply!") it is likely to have little bearing on the citizen's reluctance to comply. A more realistic explanation is that the disrespectful action represents the officer's frustration at gaining compliance and a surrender in the compliance game. An encounter level analysis would indicate that disrespect is related to noncompliance, although given the temporal ordering above the analysis would overstate such an effect. If, however, the officer were to disrespect a citizen upon entry into an encounter, we would be more confident that it may *cause* subsequent citizen noncompliance. This example illustrates the importance of reconciling the outcome of an encounter with the contours of police-citizen interaction. Assessing encounter level indicators of police behavior homogenizes the diverse paths to actions that predict subsequent citizen behavior and fails to account for differential impacts related to the point at which an officer displays a behavior .

As noted, temporal ordering is important to understanding *how* an encounter unfolds. We argue that the method of entry is an important factor in determining the outcome of police-citizen encounters (Bayley, 1986). Mastrofski and colleagues (1996) have noted that forceful entry tactics were significant predictors of noncompliance, while McCluskey et al. (1999) did not control for entry tactics. Neither study of citizen compliance examined the sequencing of police-citizen actions; rather, both treated police-citizen encounters as a whole. The current research is aimed at remedying that shortcoming.

Rather than imposing the entry, processing, and exit template on police citizen encounters, we propose to establish entry tactics as important conditioners and to divide the encounter into two phases. The first phase will include all police and citizen actions (including entry tactics) that precede the initial request for compliance. The second phase will be an identical set of items that measure officer tactics subsequent to the first request. The use of these two "phases" as reference points allows for an analysis that can pin-point where compliance requests arise, how entry tactics condition citizen responses net other interaction variables, and the effectiveness of various subsequent tactics in obtaining acquiescence from the target citizen.

The subdivision of encounters into phases also allows for the identification of two important groups; those citizens who are reluctant to comply but ultimately do, and those who are compliant in processing and ultimately rebel. We would predict that citizens are likely to remain in the same "state" throughout the encounter, especially with respect to compliance (Milgram, 1973:163) but departures from that consistency will provide an interesting basis for further investigation. The interplay of officer tactics and citizen reaction should lead to the identification of specific factors that coax citizens to obey. More importantly, this research should lead to the generation of new hypotheses about *how* officers successfully quell rebellion and act as a guide for future data collection.

Table 3.1 represents some selected results from prior analyses of citizen compliance situations. These reflect a static conception of police-citizen encounters, with the exception of entry tactics, which were included in Richmond. Our aim is to develop an understanding of how these actions unfold in the course of an encounter and their potential for stimulating different citizen reactions. By dividing, for instance, officers' use of disrespect among the aforementioned phases, we can develop insight into how it might have more powerful negative effects in phase I, when compared to its more expressive (e.g., out of frustration) uses in phase II, when a citizen has already offered an initial response to a compliance request.

Table 3.1: Comparing Selected Predictors of Compliance

Domain/Variable	Richmond Analysis	POPN Analysis
Force at Entry	-	N
Legitimating factors: Officer Showed respect	0	+
Officer showed disrespect	-	-
Officer mentions illegality	0	-

+/- = Direction of significant effect in model; N=not in that model; 0=not significant in model

Conceptualizing Citizen Compliance

Requests for compliance and the conceptualization of the idea for quantitative analysis give researchers some leeway in operationalization. Previous examples indicate that compliance is a complex phenomenon once it is taken from an abstract discourse and applied to a concrete social phenomenon.   We previously argued that compliance situations involving different targets and requestors, such as citizens and police or children and parents, might be best separated for study.   Differences *within* categories of compliance are also likely to exist.   For example, one might find different mechanisms explaining conformance with international fishing treaties when compared with treaties for keeping peace between nations (Henkin, 1979: 49-55).   In exploring police-citizen compliance we first examine several different types of police requests.   Second, we discuss the similarities and differences between the types of requests for compliance.   Third, we focus compliance in the form of on scene social control and information requests.   Finally we discuss the inherent difficulty of measuring compliance by citizens.

Police can request compliance of citizens in many settings, including cases where no face to face interaction occurs.   In a case of general compliance, the chief of police can request that all persons refrain from parking on city streets during a snow emergency, under the threat of having one's vehicle towed.   This request is not directed at specific person, but asks the general population of car owners to adjust their behavior under the threat of being towed.

Second, police can make suggestions to citizens regarding the future actions they should take to maintain their individual safety and well being.   A police officer can suggest that a victim of domestic abuse seek counsel at a local shelter.   In this situation an officer is acting in a capacity similar to a medical doctor.   He or she is attempting to modify the target's future behavior with an aim towards improving that person's "health."

Third, police can ask citizens to perform tasks for them in the context of everyday encounters.   An example would be a situation where the police ask a citizen to provide them with a license.   Such a request for information or documents can be obeyed or ignored by the citizen in question.   Citizens failing to give information are, in a sense, rebelling against the authority and legitimacy of the police (Sykes and Brent, 1980).

Finally, citizens can be asked to cease misbehavior in face-to-face contact with the police.   An officer can request, for instance, that a drunken citizen go home for the evening and sober up.   In this situation the officer could take a formal action, but chooses to allow the individual to regulate himself.

The four types of requests share an official authority as requestor and a civilian as a target. In each case the police have a legitimate interest in choosing to regulate the behavior of the citizen through requests for action. Among these situations, however, there are differences in the police-citizen dynamic. The chief's parking edict does not have a specific target or an immediacy of punishment. In that respect it has a generality similar to the legal code or the tax code; there is an articulated standard, but it is unclear whether the specific resources to enforce compliance will be forthcoming.

In the case of a referral to a domestic violence counselor the police are acting not necessarily as an authority, but as an advocate for the individual. The level of coercion that can be applied to the target is limited since the officer must instead rely on the target's perceptions of expertise. This type of situation mirrors the "paternalism with permission" found in doctor-patient relationships (Cross and Churchill, 1982), since the target is reliant on the requestor's superior knowledge and expertise. In these situations it is likely that the target's perception of the requestor's expertise would have a strong influence on the decision to comply with a stated request.

In the final example, the police are presented with a citizen who is exhibiting misbehavior, or behavior that is socially disruptive. The compliance request here is a direct substitute for legal action. The citizen is asked to refrain from a behavior or to do something that will alleviate the problem at hand. This group of requests are unique when compared to the other three types. They involve an *immediate police presence*, which distinguishes them from a general call for compliance. They represent *on scene social control*, inasmuch as the behavior being regulated goes beyond the seeking of information about an individual, but instead focuses on the behavior of the individual. Finally, unlike the cases where police, in the role of advocate, can suggest self-help, the police can bring the *full weight of their authority* to bear on this particular subset of compliance cases. A citizen who is drunk in public, for instance, can be taken to the station and placed under arrest or the police may suggest that he or she go home for the night. Citizen responses to these efforts at informally restoring order are the central focus of this research.

When the police ask for documents, such as identification, they are attempting to satisfy their need for information on which to act. Sykes and Brent (1980) explore regulation of behavior and the seeking of information as mechanisms to impose a normal or routine sequence of events in an encounter. The police can use requests for documents to glean information about their target and about the attitude of their target via the responses, but it is not a direct regulation of a "problem;" it is intended to regulate and not dispose of the encounter. Nonetheless, requesting information from a suspect also represents an intrusion into their autonomy and represents a "mild" form of compliance request that is worthy of examination. The universe of cases that are ripe for an examination of compliance, for the purposes of this study, are those which involve requests to produce identification or suspects to cease misbehavior.

Specific Compliance with Requests for Self Control

In the first set of cases identified for the current investigation we define a request for the cessation of citizen misbehavior by a police officer as the subset of compliance cases we also wish to examine. This requires a definition of "misbehavior" to capture a homogenous set of police-citizen interactions. Citizen misbehavior can take the form of clearly illegal action (i.e. meets a minimal standard set forth in a legal code). Requests to cease illegal behavior are clearly within the scope of this study. Disorderly behavior is a broad and amorphous term that is employed to describe those situations in which an individual's behavior violates a normative standard. Disorderly behaviors are typically low level offenses and represent cases where police exercise wide discretion for imposing a solution (Brown, 1988). A request for the cessation of disorderly behavior would likewise be within our definition of a request to cease misbehavior. The police also often resolve situations by separating parties in disputes and allowing for a "cooling out" period (Sherman and Berk, 1984; Stalans and Finn, 1995). This type of request goes beyond the cooperation required when a target is asked for identification. This often represents the police effort to "handle" a situation without invoking the full force of the law. We argue that forcing a citizen to leave the scene is a regulation of their behavior in an attempt to resolve the situation. Finally, the police can offer an admonishment for an individual to leave another person alone. This request recognizes the friction present and attempts to regulate it through a compliance request.

Thus, we limit specific compliance requests to four types; leave the premises, leave another person alone, cease disorderly behavior, and cease illegal behavior. We argue that these four types of requests cover the gamut of situations wherein the police use a compliance request to solve the problem confronting them in an encounter. These concepts are not mutually exclusive, however. For example, if an officer were to tell a citizen to leave the area where a restraining order is active against the target, there would be overlap among the categorical subsets of misbehavior. Clearly this is a request to leave the premises and also a request to cease illegal behavior. This does, however, support our contention that the four types of compliance requests are sufficiently broad to describe the phenomenon of interest.

Identification Compliance

The instances of "identification compliance" will capture citizen's response to police requests for their name, address, social security number, or an official document (license) to verify their identity or residence. To further narrow our sample we will focus, for purposes of identification compliance on those cases involving proactive entry in a non-traffic stop. This subset of all cases involving the request of identification in a proactive non-traffic setting is justifiable since reactive entry and traffic stops contain an inherent necessity of self-identification. By contrast, the proactive street encounter which involves an identification request is not necessarily one in which identification requests are part of a routine script (Kerner, 1968).

When is a Citizen Compliant?

Compliance, by its nature as a social phenomenon, is most easily conceptualized as a dichotomous outcome. Partial compliance implies partial noncompliance, and *any* noncompliance with an actor's request could arguably be considered as *de facto* noncompliance. An alternative approach would involve an attempt to fit some continuous measure of how much of a request was fulfilled. A continuous measure of compliance would fail to capture the meaning that is illustrated by a dichotomy bounded by requests obeyed/fulfilled or not obeyed/fulfilled by a target. But a continuous measure would allow for analysis of thresholds in target behavior. A target is conceived as compliant or noncompliant, although partial compliance is a possibility (McEwen and Maiman, 1984). Targets that ignore or refuse to do the bidding of the actor are noncompliant with respect to the request, while targets that acquiesce are compliant. Targets which partially do the bidding or promise to do as requested fall somewhere in between.

One could imagine that a promise to comply might fit either category of the dichotomy. A country, for instance, could promise to comply with international regulation by promising to open itself up for requested United Nations inspections in one week. This example, taken in its context, is likely to be perceived as an example of compliance. Conversely, a child who is requested to clean his room might promise to do it next month, a case which we would consider as noncompliant. The factor that muddies our conception of compliant/non-compliant is the time frame for future behavior. To determine whether a month is too long, one must first posit a realistic boundary on future-oriented promises to comply. Again, this is a caution to researchers who would hastily operationalize compliance. One must be cognizant that compliance, while useful for understanding myriad social behaviors, has an inherent malleability in terms of its quantification for analysis.

Determining what constitutes compliance in cases of specific compliance requests requires subjective judgment. As noted above, one could trace behavior over time and look for target behavior measured against an articulated standard. Failures would be instances where a target does not meet the standard. This conception requires a researcher to decide if failure is continuous, discrete, or captured by time to failure. That is, are all subjects who "fail" considered as equally noncompliant? Although we have no recourse to know citizen behavior beyond the face-to-face encounter, it is possible for us to determine some qualities of the target's compliance. Some targets may comply immediately, while others may openly reject the request or ignore the request, and other targets may give promises to comply in the future. These four states represent a comprehensive set of possible target responses, but their relationship to "compliance" is debatable. It is possible to order the four concepts in terms of responsiveness (Refuse, Ignore, Promise, Fully Comply) however, this scheme is unsatisfying, since some requests themselves make promises the only possible conforming response from a target. For example, an officer may ask that the citizen leave a neighbor alone in the future, to which a target can *only* respond with a promise. Such contingent requests make measuring the differences between promises and full on scene compliance difficult. The differences between ignoring police and refusing to acquiesce seem more distinct. One is a form of active rejection and the other is passive. Nevertheless, both represent noncompliant behavior and seem amenable to being viewed as more homogeneous than heterogeneous.

We argue that a citizen who makes such a promise is accepting the officer's definition of the situation. In doing so, the police are acknowledging the citizen can exercise control over the outcome if they do as promised. This is an example of police use of authority to "handle" a situation, and from our limited perspective, a target promising future compliance represents a citizen who is acquiescing. Below we attempt to quantify compliance, keeping in mind the caveats outlined above.

In cases where identification compliance has been requested there is a more easily articulated standard. Citizens either produce the requested document or information or they do not. In some cases citizens claim to not have access to a license or other document, nonetheless, they are noncompliant with the request made by the police inasmuch as they fail to produce identification. The subjective nature of "promises" to perform a behavior is removed from an examination of identification requests.

DATA COLLECTION, SITES, AND SAMPLE

The data were collected by the Project on Policing Neighborhoods (POPN) in the summer of 1996 in Indianapolis, Indiana and the summer of 1997 in St. Petersburg, Florida. These sites were selected because both were implementing community policing, both were diverse in the race and wealth of their residents, and both were receptive to hosting a large research project. Trained observers accompanied police officers for approximately 240 hours in study areas (beats) in Indianapolis and St. Petersburg. Twelve beats in each city were selected to capture a range in socioeconomic conditions. Sampled beats were matched as closely as possible across the two sites according to degree of socioeconomic distress (a summative index of the percent of families with children headed by a single female, the percent of the adult population that is unemployed, and the percent of the population that is below 50 percent of the poverty level).[1] The sample excluded those beats with the lowest socioeconomic distress so that observations would concentrate in those areas where police-citizen interactions were not infrequent. Observations were conducted at all times of the day.

During observation researchers took brief notes on police-citizen encounters, and after concluding observations they prepared computer readable data reconstructing those encounters (see Mastrofski et al., 1998, for details).[2] The coded data include citizen characteristics, police tactical choices, requests to cease misbehavior and their outcomes, location of the event, and many other descriptive variables. Observers also produced written accounts or narratives of the encounters. The narratives facilitate coding checks and establishing the sequence of officer and citizen actions within encounters. These written accounts provide the basis for coding the specific sequencing of officer actions and citizen responses in the course of the encounter. As such, they serve as a supplement to the coded data and augment our ability to measure behaviors and place them in proper order for analysis. A separate group of project researchers conducted in-person structured interviews with officers in a private space provided by the police agency. These interviews provide data on officer characteristics.

A comparison of social indicators across the two sites indicates that Indianapolis exhibits higher levels of social and economic distress (unemployment, poverty, and households with children headed by single females) than St. Petersburg, but the cities had nearly identical crime rates per capita. Because neighborhood distributions were matched as closely as possible across sites on socioeconomic distress, these differences should be minimized in the data. The per-officer crime workload was substantially higher in St. Petersburg, where staffing levels were lower. Indianapolis showed somewhat higher levels in college education and amount of training which are commonly used indicators of professionalism.

In neither department had the leadership focused specifically on achieving compliance as an alternative to formal dispositions to enforce the law and maintain order. St. Petersburg had developed an international reputation as a leader in the implementation of community policing, emphasizing "problem solving" and geographic deployment of officers and supervisors as its central features. Indianapolis's chief stressed a more diffuse approach to community policing, one that exhorted officers to engage in higher levels of "traditional" law enforcement activity (making suspect stops, arrests, and seizures of drugs and guns) to improve quality of life in the neighborhoods, as well as using alternatives, such as code enforcement to shut down problem properties. Thus, we might expect Indianapolis officers to be somewhat more sparing than their St. Petersburg counterparts in seeking compliance as an alternative to arrest.

In Indianapolis officers interacted with approximately 6,500 citizens during the observed patrol shifts, and in St. Petersburg the observed officers made contact with about 5,500 citizens. Among these contacts were brief (less than a minute) and "casual" encounters (involving no detectable policing problem), which are excluded from consideration in this study. Of the 3,172 remaining cases in Indianapolis and the 2,451 remaining cases in St. Petersburg, officers requested specific compliance of 550 and 472 citizens, respectively. Coded specific compliance requests involve any encounter in which an officer was observed requesting a citizen leave the scene or leave another person alone, cease illegal behavior, or cease disorderly behavior. Citizen responses were coded in four categories including whether the citizen ignored the officer, explicitly refused to obey, complied in presence, or promised to comply in the future. Only the final response of the citizen was captured in the database. Officers at the two sites requested specific compliance at very similar rates, 17.1 percent in Indianapolis and 18.2 percent in St. Petersburg.

An alternative strategy was used to generate a sample of proactive stops which involved the request for identification. We compiled all suspects and disputants encountered by the police, where the observed officer was in the decision making lead (n=3,128) then eliminated those that were involved in encounters that were coded as traffic stops or involved reactive police contact (e.g. a response to a call). The coded data from the Project on Policing Neighborhoods, collected by trained observers, allowed us to perform a computer selection of these cases. Of all citizens encountered there were 793 cases in which the problem was not a traffic stop and the police made a self initiated contact with the citizen. To further narrow the sample we entered the narrative data into a database program and searched for text strings for the words "license" and "identification," including misspellings and truncations that the field researchers were known to use.

This search narrowed the number of cases to 450 instances where police initiated a non-traffic encounter and may have made a request for a license or identification. Upon examining this group of cases we found 343 citizens (200 from Indianapolis, and 143 from St. Petersburg) who were asked for identification or licenses; of that number, 319 had a narrative that was sufficiently detailed to provide a basis for coding and complete information from the coded POPN data.

Twenty-two cases were discarded because the narrative was not adequate for determining whether the citizen cooperated or was inadequate for the purposes of coding other variables and three cases had missing observational data. One concern with this method for identifying cases is that we may have performed an insufficient text search on the cases, but an examination of a small sample of cases in which key search terms were not found revealed no instance of a request for identification from a suspect. Therefore we conclude that the boundary drawn around these kinds of encounters (proactive, non-traffic, identification requested) has been adequately enumerated through this process.

Measuring Compliance

Ideally we would be able to track citizen behavior subsequent to compliance requests over a period of time. Citizen conformance could be measured in terms of "survival" as a compliant citizen. Conformance could also be measured in terms of the internalization of the request. The psychometric approach might rely on Kelman's (1958) extension of compliance from its behavioral manifestation to the cognitive levels of internalization and identification that a change agent might try to achieve. Here one would stress how citizen's attitudes change after the request for compliance is made. While both of these approaches would yield useful results, neither is practical for the present investigation, in which observation of the target is limited to observable actions and is temporally limited to the time the police and citizen spend face-to-face in an encounter.

We propose measuring compliance as a dichotomous outcome, measured at two time points in the face to face encounter. Herein we have isolated a small component of compliance for the present study: First our interest centers on those cases where an officer requests a citizen to leave another person alone, to leave the premises, to cease disorderly behavior, or to cease illegal behavior in the sample of 1,022 sample cases. Second, we focus on the sample of 343 proactive stops where police ask suspects for identification. Noncompliance results when a citizen has failed to acquiesce or ignores that type of request at the end of a phase. On the other hand, compliance is achieved when an individual fulfills an officer's request or promises to do so at the conclusion of a phase.

As indicated previously two dichotomous compliance scores were generated for citizens in each sample. The first indicates the response to the *first* request made by the police in the course of the encounter. The second indicates the *end state* of the encounter, or, more precisely, whether the citizen is in conformance with all of the police's stated demands upon conclusion of the interaction. Below we briefly illustrate the coding of phase I outcomes for each dependent measure, but we reserve a more complete treatment of phase I and phase II coding for the chapters that address these questions.

Citizen Compliance with Police Requests for Self-Control

Our first dependent variable is a binary measure of citizen compliance with the first request for self-control during the police-citizen encounter. Those citizens who comply on scene (212, or 23 percent of the sample) or promise to comply (439, or 47 percent) with the police request are considered compliant and are coded as one. Citizens who ignore the police request (137, or 15 percent) or refuse to obey (151, or 16 percent) are considered noncompliant and are coded as zero. For the sample 69 percent of the citizens were compliant in phase I of the encounter.

Citizen Compliance with Police Requests for Identification

The measure of compliance with requests for identification is similar to that discussed for self control requests. Here we also consider cooperative behavior as sufficient for being compliant. For instance, citizens may offer alternate forms of identification to police and that, we argue, should be considered cooperative behavior. For example, a police officer asking a suspect for a license might instead receive verbal information regarding the suspect's social security number, address, or an alternative form of identification. In this analysis we consider that as an example of cooperative citizen behavior. Only in cases of refusal, totally putting off the request, or ignoring the officer do we consider the request to be one of non-compliance. The dependent variable that we examine first is the citizen's response to a police officer's initial request for identification. In 21 percent of the 319 cases with valid data the target citizen ignored or refused to provide information to the police.

Generalizability to the Universe of Compliance Requests

We have noted that there are a variety of possible requests that police make of citizens. One mechanism for assessing how the two types of requests that we have chosen for analysis fit into that larger universe is to enumerate all possible requests made of citizens. To accomplish this we conducted limited analysis of data from the Project on Policing Neighborhoods to examine the prevalence, frequency, and outcomes of requests of 100 police-suspect encounters. The data for these cases were drawn from narratives generated by observers in the Project on Policing Neighborhoods. The accounts were considered data sources from which we could ascertain what types of requests police make of citizens during encounters.

To analyze our sample of police-suspect encounters we generated a list of all requests noted in the narratives and citizen responses to the requests. Results are presented in table 3.2. In examining these encounters we found that in only two cases were there no apparent requests for compliance of any type documented in the narrative. The modal number of compliance requests of any type in the sample was two and the average number was 3.75 requests per suspect. Since we are proposing coding data from narratives that observers did not code we have only one comparison to make with their data: Whether they coded a compliance request or not in the sample. Our data compare favorably with 75 percent concordance and a moderate Kappa reliability statistic in this sample of 100 cases.

Table 3.2 Distribution of compliance requests in a sample of encounters (100 cases)

Request Type	Min.	Max.	Total Requests	Mean	S.D.	Prevalence Type (%)
Any Request Type	0	13	375	3.75	2.83	98
Request for Information	0	12	242	2.42	2.43	85
Request for On-Scene behavior	0	6	89	0.89	1.25	45
Request for Self Control	0	3	44	0.44	0.67	36

Three broad categories of requests emerged from the analysis of the sample narratives: Requests for information (which include requests for identification), requests for some on scene behavior, and requests to exercise self-control as a resolution to the presenting situation (such as leaving the premises). A detailed breakdown of all request types can be found in table 3.3. The most prevalent was the request for information from the citizen. These request types were present in 85 percent of the encounters and there was an average of 2.4 information requests per encounter in the sample. The modal number of requests for information was one, and the number of information requests made in the course of the encounter ranged from zero to twelve. A total of ten distinct categories were identified as requests for compliance with regards to giving police information. Three types of information emerged as those most often requested by police: Personal information about the suspect such as identity, date of birth, and social security number was requested in 47 percent of the cases. Justification of the suspect's actions or an explanation of actions was requested in 33 percent of the cases. Finally, general probes of the citizens' knowledge about the situation were present in 24 percent of the cases.

The second type of request was one for on scene behavioral regulation, such as standing in a certain area, waiting for the officer, or submitting to police control (e.g. allowing oneself to be handcuffed or placed in a police cruiser) at least one of which occurred in 45 percent of the cases. The average number of behavioral requests in the sample was .89. The modal number of requests for on scene behavioral compliance was zero, and the number of these requests ranged from zero to six. A total of twelve distinct categories were identified to capture requests for on scene behavioral regulation. Two primary categories of request emerged from the sample: Requests for the citizen to stop or wait were present in 32 percent of the sample. Submission to on scene police request for physical control, such as waiting in the cruiser or being handcuffed, occurred in seven percent of the sample cases.

The third type of compliance request made by police comprised efforts to get citizens to exercise self control as a resolution to the presenting situation (leave premises, cease misbehavior). These request types were present in 36 percent of the sample encounters, and on average there were .44 requests made per encounter. The modal number of requests was zero, and the number of self control requests made in a single case ranged from zero to three. Four categories of behavior were subsumed under this grouping, but two primary requests emerged. The first was requests to leave the premises, which were made in 15 percent of the cases. The second was requests to cease illegal behavior, which were made in 13 percent of the cases.

Table 3.3 Prevalence and total of request types in sample encounters

	Prevalence	Total Number
Requests for Information by police		
Identity, age, SS#, license, address	47	66
Justification of actions	33	58
Probe knowledge of situation	24	34
Justification of presence	18	32
Knowledge about compliance with laws	16	17
Prior behavioral history	14	15
Give information about someone else	7	8
How can situation be resolved?	5	5
Confess to an action	2	6
Miscellaneous	1	1
On scene behavior requests by police		
Wait or stop	32	52
Submit to police control (e.g. handcuffing)	7	8
Calm self down	5	6
Perform administrative task	4	4
Recognize consequences of behavior	2	2
Submit to search	2	2
Get help for self	2	3
Allow police to get involved in situation	2	3
Asked to seek help from third party	2	2
Asked to perform a task on scene	2	4
Separate from another person at scene	1	2
Give help to other citizen at scene	1	1
Self Control Requests by police		
Leave premises	15	16
Cease illegal behavior/correct illegal situation	13	15
Cease disorderly behavior/ fix nuisance situation	7	9
Leave another person alone	2	4

The rates of compliance with different types of requests in the sample were also assessed. Citizens were in total compliance with 87 percent of the information requests, 78 percent of the on scene behavioral regulation requests, and 89 percent of the self-control requests. The distribution of noncompliance in the self control sample does not comport with the distribution in the larger sample where we find, according to our analysis of the phase I sample, noncompliance in 31 percent of the cases.

Nevertheless the analysis of this sample does allow us to assess the relationship of the types of compliance requests we intend to study and those that exist in everyday encounters with suspects. With respect to requests for identification, it seems that they belong in the most common category and are the most prevalent type of information requested of citizens, which is of little surprise (e.g. Sykes and Brent, 1980). The frequency of on scene regulation, which occurred in forty-five percent of the sample cases cannot be directly compared to the data coded by observers or the dependent variable studied in this research. Interestingly, these types of requests have some overlap with the dependent variable, in terms of the relationship to self-control. Requesting that a person recognize the consequences of his behavior, for example, or submitting to police control could be subsumed under a larger framework of "self-control". Finally the self-control requests identified in 36 cases were found to fit within the four categories proposed—leave premises, leave another alone, cease disorderly behavior, cease illegal behavior. The broad nature of "cease disorderly behavior," however, subsumes a variety of actions. Future conceptualizations of the dependent variable, involving other research questions might benefit from a broader conceptualization of compliance requests for self-control, as well as more specific categorizations of compliance requests than those in this study. For the question posed by this research, however, the conceptualization appears adequate and sufficiently broad to capture whether a request for self-control was made, if not the precise nature of that request.

CHAPTER 4
PREDICTING COMPLIANCE

This research encompasses two variations on police requests for compliance. The first treats requests for self-control as a dependent variable and the second treats requests for licenses, in street stops, as the dependent variable. This presents the quandary of establishing measures for analysis that are substantially different in their distributions and somewhat different in the coding rules adopted to capture variables (for example, asking for a license is an independent variable in one analysis, and a dependent variable in another). In addition, actions that officers and citizens take are coded at two points in time; first, they are assessed in the period prior to the police's first request for compliance (Phase I), and then they are assessed subsequent to that initial request (Phase II). Variables that are static (citizen age, citizen race, etc.) are only measured at the beginning of the encounter.

Below we present an exhaustive list of variables used in the analyses, accompanied by coding conventions. A set of coding rules is included in the Appendix to establish the face validity of the coding process and to precisely note what coders attended to in making their decisions.

Coding was done by researchers scanning observers' written narratives; hence, we present this chapter as a general introduction to the independent measures, their construction, and their reliability, when they were coded from the narratives. Reliability of the observers' coded data is predicated on a systematic training regime as outlined by Mastrofski and colleagues (1998). The treatment of each measure will be addressed in the chapters reporting the separate analyses as well, but there we will focus more on the distribution within each sample analyzed.

An item by item comparison of the author's coding and an independent coder's assessment of the police-citizen interaction is reported for each variable that was hand coded from the narrative data in phase I of a sample of 104 randomly chosen encounters where self-control was requested. Variables will be introduced in terms of the domains that they represent. The descriptions below refer to phase I coding, but the phase II measures are essentially identical except for their timing in the police-citizen encounter.

ASSESSING RELIABILITY OF HAND-CODED ITEMS

As noted, a variety of independent measures used in this study are coded out of the narrative accounts compiled by the POPN researchers. The rules for constructing these measures appear in the Appendix and detail how coding decisions should be made with respect to the different variables that were coded across both phases of each encounter. The coding rules for these items erred on the side of cautious interpretation inasmuch as the narrative had to contain clear indication of a police action, and unless noted no observer coding judgments were adopted. Thus, the reliability of the coding rules as they apply to the narrative data must be assessed when a variable has been coded out of the written narratives. Since both phases of the encounter draw upon identical sets of measures, it was determined that assessing the reliability of the coding rules for Phase I cases would be adequate and the level of reliability achieved across the two encounter phases would likely be similar if not identical.

To check the reliability of the coding schemes we randomly sampled approximately ten percent of all 1,022 cases, which amounted to 104 cases from that population. The 104 narratives involving sample suspects were then assembled into machine-readable files. An independent coder, a Michigan State University Criminal Justice graduate student, was hired and trained for one day on how the coding rules were to be applied to the narratives as well as the conventions associated with interpreting the narratives. These conventions include shorthand used to identify participants (C1 is citizen one in the coded data, C2 is citizen two) and the fact that the narratives were not always "linear" stories, but required complete reading to determine the sequence of events, before attempting to read the narratives and code data. The codes for phase I of these cases, based on the coding scheme, were then generated by the independent coder over the course of the following week on the first 56 cases sampled. After completing that sample coding discrepancies were discussed in a session in which several coding rules and narrative conventions were reviewed. The second set of 48 cases was then completed by the independent coder. The original cases were merged with the independent coder's cases and the percentage of concordance in the independent measures was assessed.

We use Cohen's (1960) Kappa to gauge the reliability of each of our measures that are coded from narrative data. One assumption of Kappa is that the coders have equal skill and training in applying the coding rules to observations (Cohen, 1960). The cumbersome nature of the narrative conventions, coupled with the complex coding scheme used to collect these data suggests that the independent coder's second wave of data collection (n=48) might be more reliable than the first wave (n=56). If the Kappa increases in the second wave, then we argue that those reliability coefficients from the first sample are partially an artifact of differences in coder experience. For measures with Kappa statistics at or below .5 we computed (where possible) a second Kappa statistic from the second wave of coding to determine whether a "learning curve" is a plausible explanation for the generation of the low reliability statistic. The second Kappa is reported, if necessary, in the tables in the K_2 row.

The logic of our presentation will be to address each domain of independent variables that we will incorporate in our analyses. All variables are presented in table 4.1, and those that are not included in the reliability check have no statistics reported. Below we report the results of those comparisons for each of the independent measures coded within the narratives.

Entry Tactics

Entry tactics are measured along a continuum of coerciveness. We adopt a set of police actions that includes passive interaction (i.e. wherein the police do not assert their authority in any fashion), questioning, verbal requests, verbal commands or threats, and forceful physical or legal entry as the initial police action starting an encounter. It is possible to allow these to be arrayed in the form of a continuum from least coercive to most coercive or to code each as a separate dummy variable (the latter is reviewed in this section, since reliability is assessed according to the coding of dummy measures). Entry tactics represent police tactics at the beginning of an encounter and can be directed at any citizen, and are not restricted to the compliance target. The purpose of coding entry tactics is to ascertain the effects of this initial self-presentation to the compliance target. We measure entry tactics as the first action taken by police in the target's presence at the beginning of encounters. Entry tactics were assessed using six dummy measures including whether the officer was passive, asked questions, issued commands, used threats, used physical force, or arrested the citizen upon first contact. Table 4.1 presents the concordance rate for each separate type of entry tactic recorded by the coders. The three most forceful entry tactics had near universal agreement among coders, and the three least forceful tactics had greater than 85 percent agreement on each category. Cohen's Kappa coefficients indicate that each of the entry tactics is reliably captured since all are well above the .40 level set by Landis and Koch (1977) as moderate and all but passive entry cross the .60 level above which one interprets the kappa coefficient as indicating substantial reliability.

Indicators of Procedural Justice

All indicators of procedural justice are coded in both Phase I and Phase II of the police citizen interaction. This aids in determining the effect on initial decisions to comply and the overall decision-making of the citizen. The measures we use to represent various dimensions of procedurally just processing were coded entirely from the narrative data. These represent a variety of measures of citizen and officer behaviors that can be compared for reliability across coders. Unless noted otherwise, a dummy coding strategy (1=presence of the condition, 0=absence of the condition) was adopted for coding items from the narrative.

A pair of procedural justice indicators captures the citizen's perception of the police's moral authority to intervene. Citizen targets that make verbal statements that are supportive or complementary of the police are conceived of as believing in the rectitude of the police presence and actions. Similarly, target statements that are derogatory and disrespectful, question the police authority, or challenge the right to intervene (not including noncompliant acts) are coded as verbalizations of immorality. The former represent a cache of good will that is likely to engender compliance, the latter represents a cauldron of animosity that could erupt in noncompliant behavior if police do not defuse it.

The coding of these items is restricted to citizen "entry" tactics. That is the citizen must take an action specified above prior to any police tactic. The valence represented by these measures is a proxy for pre-existing opinions of authorities, which may affect the interpretation of other police actions. Both measures have near perfect inter rater concordance at 99 percent agreement. Unfortunately, Kappa statistics are not computable due to the limited variance in the measures.

Disrespectful and respectful police behavior was coded from the narrative accounts. When police attacked a citizen's identity (e.g. use of expletives, disparaging remarks, slurs) they were considered disrespectful. When the police were characterized as being polite and responsive to targets they were coded as respectful. It is possible for the police to have been both respectful and disrespectful in the course of an encounter, or they may have exhibited signs of neither respect nor disrespect towards a target during an encounter. Leventhal's (1980) concept of ethicality is captured by the quality of treatment citizens receive at the hands of police, with respect being a sign of more ethicality and disrespect being a sign of less ethicality. Authorities that are more *ethical* are more likely to be obeyed.

Also noted previously, "voice" is an important component of procedural justice theory. We propose the construction of two dummy variables, coded within each phase, to measure the effects of voice on subsequent decisions to comply. A dummy variable is coded to indicate that a target had an opportunity to tell his or her side of the story. We consider citizens that communicate facts about the presenting situation to the police to have had an opportunity to exercise their voice. A dummy variable is also coded to capture whether the police cut the target out of the processing of the encounter, by silencing him or her through a command. Regardless of whether this occurred because a citizen is speaking out of turn, or because the police are being uncivil, such a silencing should hypothetically produce the same voice effect.

We expect respectful treatment and the opportunity to exercise one's "voice" to be positively related to compliance, since they promote the idea that the target's perspective is valuable to the police. Conversely the indicators for termination of voice and disrespectful treatment should be negatively related to compliance since this is likely lead to undermining the legitimacy of subsequent compliance requests thus reducing the likelihood of citizens fulfilling those requests.

The four measures, outlined above, that comport with "ethicality" and the dimension of "representation" with regard to procedurally just processing were compared across coders to determine reliability. Each of the measures is over 80 percent in terms of simple inter rater agreement. The Kappa statistics for disrespect and whether the citizen had an opportunity to voice his or her side of the story indicate substantial agreement. The Kappa statistics for respect and whether voice was terminated both indicated moderate agreement levels between coders. Using the Kappa statistic to compare only second wave cases, for the latter two measures, indicates that both show a marked improvement in agreement, including perfect concordance for our measure of the termination of voice.

Three of our procedural justice measures are based around information seeking by the police. These measures are used to capture information seeking including whether the police sought information about the person, information about the presenting situation, or information about the solution of the presenting problem. Three dummy variables were coded to capture those cases where police actively sought information from the target. One captures whether police seek the identity of the individual (which will be excluded from the analysis of identification compliance since it is a constant). The second captures whether police ask the citizen/target directly for information regarding the presenting situation, such as what has occurred or who is involved. A third information seeking variable that we capture is whether the police ask the citizen about how the presenting situation ought to be resolved. We expect that as police demonstrate that the target's input is valued then the likelihood of compliance with a request will increase.

All three measures have simple inter rater concordance rates greater than 90 percent. The Kappa statistics for police seeking information on identity (.92) and police seeking information on the situation (.77) indicate substantial to near perfect reliability. Kappa statistics could not be generated for the measure of police information seeking concerning a solution to the problem since it was rare and hence the variation was limited. The simple percent of concordant cases was, however, nearly perfect.

When citizens perceive bias or partisanship, or a lack of carefully reasoned decision-making on the part of authorities they are less likely to comply. If the police clearly take sides in a dispute or base a decision largely on one party's desires, they are likely to be perceived as being partisans. We will code two dichotomous variables for each phase to capture whether police are acting in a biased fashion. The first will indicate if officers are acting against the target at the behest of another. To code this in the affirmative it is necessary that it be clearly indicated in verbal statements by the officer(s). For example, an officer would have to indicate that "X told us that you [the target] should leave for the night. Why don't you?" The second variable will capture those instances where police base their decisions regarding the target on their own personal authority or the authority of the law. This, again, requires evidence of clear articulation that the law is the basis for the decision. An example of such an indication might be "X [target], there is a restraining order against you, it requires that I ask that you leave this person alone." The former indicator is likely to be associated with rebellion, since the target could perceive unfairness when the police are acting as an agent of another party. Conversely, when it is evident that the police have based their decisions firmly in a personal evaluation of the situation or with respect to the law, the target is more likely to perceive the treatment as fair.

A third variable, closely related to those reflecting bias, is one that captures how the police weigh their decision against the limits of their authority. This is also a dummy coded variable which will represent those cases where police clearly indicate that the legal attributes of the situation allow them to make an arrest, issue a citation, inform a parent of the target's behavior but that they will impose a lesser burden on the citizen. This reflects, in theory, evidence of police weighing the situation and citizen behaviors to generate an alternative resolution, which should increase the likelihood of compliance with specific requests. This measure is available only for specific requests and not for requests for identification, however, the likelihood of an identification request being preceded by such a police action seems to be limited. In all compliance cases it is likely that no standard will be clearly articulated in most encounters, since police often issue orders without noting they are basing it on law, personal evaluation of the situation, or the desires of the third party. This "gray area" where the police do not communicate the basis of action to the target is the reference category. Using this category for contrasts, we would still expect biased/partisan decisions to be more likely to result in noncompliance, and those firmly rooted in law or careful decision-making to be seen as justifiable and more likely to result in compliance than those that are not firmly rooted in either extreme.

All three measures of decision making (or impartiality, depending on one's interpretation of the fit between these actions and the concepts outlined by Tyler, Lind and Leventhal) have simple inter rater concordance rates greater than 85 percent. Kappa statistics generated for whether the decision is rooted in leniency indicated substantial inter rater reliability. Our measure of whether the police based their decision on legal grounds was, in the full sample, only moderately reliable with a Kappa of .44. Reanalysis of the sample using only wave two cases from the independent coder yielded a Kappa of .79 indicating that there was substantial agreement between coders. Finally, our measure of whether the police showed bias in their decision-making had perfect concordance and generated a perfect Kappa statistic.

Finally, we measure probable cause or the level of evidence of wrongdoing by the citizen; a variable that is a proxy for the morality or rectitude of police presence. Whether police had probable cause to stop the citizen, which would influence the legitimacy of their presence at the scene, was measured as being present when the evidence level rises to two or more points from the following list (scores in parentheses): officer observes violation (2), officer obtains physical evidence implicating citizen (2), officer hears full confession (2), officer hears eyewitness testimony implicating citizen (1), officer hears partial confession (1). Mastrofski and colleagues (1996) originally developed this as a seven point evidence scale and it has been refined to reflect probable cause for arrest when the level of evidence rises above a two on his original scale. The inter rater concordance is nearly ninety percent and the Kappa statistic of .75 indicates that the measure has substantial reliability.

Indicators of Coercion

Coercive power that is brought against a citizen, as well as his or her capacity to resist, may influence the decision to comply with police requests. We measure fourteen variables that represent the coercive power that police have applied (commands, threats, arrest, etc.), the ability of citizens to resist (possession of weapons), and the coercive context of the encounter (numbers of civilian and police bystanders). Below we discuss the construction of each and where necessary note the reliability of the measures derived from narrative data.

The set of variables that measure coercion in the police-citizen encounter, presented in table 4.1, includes actions citizens and police may take in the first phase of interaction. These include mentioning arresting the target citizen, mentioning citing the target citizen, making suggestions or requests of the target, commanding the target, threatening the target, or using physical force against the target which were coded from the narrative data using dummy variables (1=presence of the action, 0=absence of the action). The percentage of concordant cases on these six indicators is over 90 percent for each except whether police suggested or requested something from the target, which had concordant observations in 86 percent of the cases.

The Kappa statistics obtained for these comparisons indicate that five of the six are within the range of moderate to almost perfect using the Landis and Koch (1977) criteria. The variable measuring suggestions and requests is at an unacceptable level of .37, which indicates only a fair correspondence between coders beyond chance. Examining the second wave of independent coding for requests and suggestions we obtained a Kappa statistic of .50, indicating that there was moderate agreement above chance for the two coders.

Table 4.1 also illustrates the inter rater correspondence on four police actions, handcuffing, searching, arresting, or citing the target. These were coded from the narratives using dummy measures (1=presence of the action, 0=absence of the action). Each of these measures generated an inter rater concordance above 95 percent for the sample cases. The Kappa statistic also indicates that the inter rater reliability for all of the measures is moderate to near perfect. Whether the compliance target had a weapon, a citizen behavior (or condition), was coded from the narratives and simple concordance was 99 percent for this measure, and a Kappa of .85 indicates almost perfect reliability. The type of initial compliance request is also coded as being an authoritative (commands, threats) or nonauthoritative (suggestions, requests, negotiation, etc.) request for compliance. No independent coding of this variable was undertaken, but the concordance of other measures of coercion (entry tactics, for example) indicates that we can have some confidence in the accuracy and reliability of its coding.

Within this domain we use three variables that are constructed from the electronic data recorded by the POPN researchers. Gender dyad is a variable measuring the gender relationship between the target (citizen) and the requestor (lead police officer) (1=female target/male requestor, 2=target/requestor same gender, 3=male target/female requestor). The variable transforms the conceptualization of gender, as a representation of coercive balance of power, as suggest by Katz (1988). This conceptualization is a variation on a coding scheme to capture relative status of citizens who request action of police in previous research by Mastrofski, Snipes, Parks, and Maxwell (2000). This is constructed from the coded data collected by the observers regarding the gender of the citizen and surveys conducted by POPN researchers that coded the gender of the observed officer. The number of police on scene at the time of the initial request for compliance is coded, in the form of a count, from the observation data originally collected by the POPN observers. The larger police presence is hypothesized to represent a greater amount of coercive force available to subdue a resistant target. The size of the citizen audience, including bystanders, is also measured using the count of the audience coded by on scene assessment of the POPN observers.

Third Party Influences

To capture the effects that the actions of civilian third parties can have on the interaction between police and citizens, we measure four variables in both Phase I and Phase II. First, a pair of dummy variables capture third parties that suggest that the target be cooperative or place police presence in a positive light or suggest that the target be uncooperative with the police or cast the police in a negative light. A third dummy variable captures whether there is a third party who is, himself or herself, uncooperative with the police. When a third party fails to cooperate with the police or is disrespectful towards them we consider that a case of third party rebellion. A fourth dummy variable captures whether a "third-party" citizen was asked for self-control and complied. Overall, third parties supporting conforming action or using words supporting the authorities should have a positive influence on the target's decision to comply. Conversely, words encouraging nonconforming behavior or a third party's resistant behavior should have a negative impact on the target's decision to comply.

Another dimension of the situation that reflects on the legitimacy of police intervention is the presence of an adversary, relatives, or an adversary that is related to the compliance target. We measure whether there was an adversary present and whether that adversary was related to the target with two dummy variables. Situations involving an unrelated adversary are likely to result in compliant behavior since the police and adversary are aligned against the target and represent a coercive force. Conversely, if the adversary is related to the target the legitimacy of a compliance request may be questioned. The nature of adversaries' effect on target compliance is, in theory, conditionally impacted by the relationship between the target and adversary, thus requiring several measures to disentangle the effects.

A total of seven third party factors were hand coded, using dummy variables, from the narratives and are presented in table 4.1. Two measure whether citizens were present who were either compliant or noncompliant with police requests. Two measure the valence of verbalization from third parties including whether they make positive comments or negative comments about the police presence. Three measure whether an adversary is present, whether a relative is present, whether a relative is in the role of adversary. From the reference point of simple percentage concordance five are above 90 percent concordance, and the sixth, third party noncompliant is 84 percent concordant. Kappa statistics for each of the variables indicate that there is moderate to substantial reliability between coders in all but two variables. Third party positive verbalizations and third party compliance with police requests have questionable levels of reliability according to the computed Kappa statistics. Further examination of the sub sample of second wave reliability cases was conducted for the variables capturing whether a third party made positive comments on police presence and whether a third party was compliant on scene (which was below .50 but was rounded up in Table 4.1). The Kappa statistic computed on the second wave of cases capturing third party compliance rose to .73, indicating substantial inter rater reliability. Due to high concordance and limited variation no corresponding statistic could be generated for whether third parties made positive verbalizations.

Table 4.1 Independent Measures and Phase I Reliability

Independent Measures	Coders Agree	Coders Disagree	% Agree	K_1	K_2
Police Entry					
Passive	95	9	91	.59	
Ask Questions	90	14	87	.72	
Command	93	11	89	.67	
Threat	104	0	100	a	
Physical Force	103	1	99	.8	
Arrest	104	0	100	1	
Procedural Justice					
Citizen Entry (Rectitude)	103	1	99	b	
Citizen Entry (Morality)	103	1	99	b	
Police Respect Citizen	85	19	82	.5	.57
Police Disrespect Citizen	99	5	95	.71	
Citizen has Voice	90	14	87	.71	
Citizen's Voice Terminated	100	4	96	.48	1.0
Police Seek Information: Identity	100	4	96	.92	
Police Seek Information: Situation	93	11	89	.77	
Police Seek Information: Solution	102	2	98	b	
Police Indicate Bias	104	0	100	1	
Police Indicate Leniency	92	12	89	.62	
Police Indicate Independence	97	7	93	.44	.79
Police have Probable Cause	92	12	89	.75	
Police Coercion					
Police Mention Arrest	98	6	94	.84	
Police Make Suggestion	89	15	86	.37	.50
Police Command	94	10	90	.65	
Police Threaten	99	5	95	.59	
Citizen Handcuffed	103	1	99	.92	
Citizen Searched	99	5	95	.58	
Physical Force v Citizen	103	1	99	.85	
Gender Dyad	x	x	x	x	
Citizen Arrested	103	1	99	.66	
Citizen Cited	103	1	99	.8	

Independent Measures	Coders Agree	Coders Disagree	% Agree	K_1	K_2
Citizen has Weapon	103	1	99	.85	
Number of Police Present (sqrt)	x	x	x	x	
Number of Citizens Present (sqrt)	x	x	x	x	
Police Command Self Control	c	c	c	c	
Third Party Influences					
3rd Party Positive Verbalization	101	3	97	.39	b
3rd Party Negative Verbalization	103	1	99	.85	
3rd Party Rebellion	87	17	84	.59	
3rd Party Compliant	97	7	93	.50	.73
Relative is Adversary	100	4	96	.83	
Adversary Present	99	5	95	.87	
Relative Present	97	7	93	.55	
Key Citizen/Officer Characteristics					
Indicators of Irrationality	x	x	x	x	x
Citizen Age	x	x	x	x	x
Officer Minority	x	x	x	x	x
Citizen Minority	x	x	x	x	x
Citizen Low Income	x	x	x	x	x

[a]No threats issued in sample of 104 cases; kappa cannot be estimated
[b] Kappa not computable for these cases due to limited variance
[c]Level of request omitted from the reliability check
[x]Measure taken from observation or interview data collected by POPN researchers

Citizen and Officer Characteristics

Static citizen characteristics are assessed at the beginning of the encounter regardless of the phase analyzed. Variables for five characteristics were coded out of the electronic POPN data. Observers made the initial judgment of citizen wealth inferred from possessions and the ability to maintain a minimal standard of living based on clothing, residence, and verbal statements by the citizen. As such, we include a dummy variable that captures the level of wealth that a citizen possesses. Those who are unable to maintain a minimum standard of living are coded using a dummy variable representing lower class status. Citizen race, also based on observer's judgments, is measured using a dummy variable to capture the minority status of the compliance target. Race of the police officer is coded as a dummy variable (0=minority, 1=white) based on a self-reported survey, and if not available in that format, it was based on the judgment of the POPN observer. The youthfulness of the citizen was assessed on scene by observers, and was measured by an eight category variable. This variable subdivides chronological age into eight broad categories (1=5 and under; 2=6-12 years; 3=13-17; 4=18-20; 5=21-29; 6=30-44; 7=45-59; 8=60 and above).

Measures of irrationality rely on the observer's assessment of the target on three dimensions. First, observers coded whether the citizen was under the influence of strong emotions in the form of anger or depression. Training and guidelines indicated that the citizen had to exhibit signs of anger (shouting, red face, gritted teeth) or depression (crying, frowning) at the beginning of the encounter to be coded as such. Second, they assessed whether the citizen exhibited behavioral signs of the effects of alcohol or other drugs. This is based on observing slurred speech and motor impairment in the citizen. Third, observers indicated whether the target was affected by apparent mental illness. This latter characteristic is likely to be somewhat unreliable, since it is likely based on information communicated from third parties, the citizens, and the police themselves (e.g., Engle and Silver, 2001). The measure of alcohol/drug use represents a clearly observable phenomenon, and unless a citizen-target was particularly adept at functioning in an intoxicated state, the observed characteristics were likely to be reliably coded. Similarly, the expression of emotion is observable, and lest the target was passing as a calm citizen (which would indicate a measure of self-control) we are confident that this too is reliably measured. Taken together the presence of a greater number of these three factors is likely to impair the judgment and rational functioning of a citizen target. Thus, we constructed an index of irrational behavior similar to those used by Mastrofski and colleagues (1996) and McCluskey et al. (1999). The presence of irrationality is likely to undermine the predictive power of coercive police actions, and actions that were judged to be fair and just in the objective sense. The estimation of models where indicators of irrationality are present and absent is likely to be a useful step in conducting the present inquiry. It is conceivable that irrational targets are wholly incapable of using police tactics and other situational factors as cues to accurately guide behavior and has an interactive effect on other indicators in the model. Coercion that would subdue "rational"actors may instead incite rebellion among the irrational (e.g. Pernanen, 1992).

Social Ecological Context

Sampson, Raudenbush, and Earls (1997) have elaborated on the "concentrated disadvantage" that exists in some neighborhoods. Rather than rely on the additive effects of the three predictors that Shaw and McKay suggest, these authors insist that effects are multiplicative. Concentrated disadvantage crumbles the social bonds that informally control citizens.

Reisig and Parks (2001) analyzed data from St. Petersburg and Indianapolis that indicate that concentrated disadvantage, which is a proxy for macro-level informal social control, can be measured through an index of the percent female headed households with children, the percent minority, the percent of people below poverty level, the percent under the age of eighteen, and the percent of persons unemployed in a geographic unit. The indicator of concentrated disadvantage should be negatively associated with citizen compliance, since in our theoretical framework, deviant behavior is more likely to occur in areas where informal social control is lacking (e.g., Morenoff, Sampson, and Raudenbush, 2002).

CONCLUSION

The measures captured using the coding scheme appear to be reliable according to our inter rater comparisons using the random sample of 104 cases coded by the independent coder. All measures had concordance rates above 80 percent in terms of simple percentage comparisons. With respect to the statistical assessment of the inter rater reliability using the Kappa statistic the measures had, at minimum, moderate inter rater reliability according to the benchmarks noted by Landis and Koch (1977). The two exceptions were whether police requested or suggested the target citizen do something (k=.37) and whether a third party made a positive comment about the police on scene (k=.39). Of the 34 Kappa statistics produced using the total sample, 22, or 65 percent, could be interpreted as indicating substantial or almost perfect inter rater reliability according to the Landis and Koch criteria.

The reliability tests serve three important purposes with respect to present and future research. First, they support the inference that the data produced for analysis in this study are themselves reliably coded from the POPN narrative data. Second, the strong concordance between the original coder and the independent coder indicate that the coding rules developed in the Appendix are useful tools for future researchers desiring to replicate these measures. Third, by noting the lower reliability for first wave measures assessed by the independent coder, we are able to caution future researchers about the existence of a "learning curve" inherent in the interpretation of POPN narratives and the need for coders to be trained thoroughly before being allowed to produce data for analysis.[1]

CHAPTER FIVE

COMPLIANCE REQUESTS FOR SELF-CONTROL

This chapter is focused on police requests for suspects to control themselves with respect to ceasing disorderly behaviors, ceasing illegal behaviors, leaving the scene, or leaving another person alone. We will first describe the overall sample of police-citizen encounters. The dependent measure will then be described as well as the independent measures within the various domains that we have hypothesized as having an impact on citizens' decisions to comply. This will be repeated to address the multi-phasic nature of police-citizen encounters that we have previously described. We will examine the independent measures in the order of entry tactics, procedural justice indicators, coercive power indicators, and key characteristics of officers and citizens. Finally, we will build models of citizen compliance using several strategies to determine the factors that impact a citizen's decision to comply. As mentioned previously our independent measures are captured up to the point where the police make the initial request for compliance. The phase I dependent variable is the citizen's response to the police request for self-control. A similar approach will then be taken to describe and analyze the police-citizen encounters to be analyzed for phase II.

We drew our sample of study cases from the Project on Policing Neighborhoods' coded data. Observers noted whether a compliance request was made during the encounter. We selected those cases where observers coded the event and limited the sample to those cases where the observed officer was responsible for taking the decision-making lead during the encounter (which allows us to include pertinent officer characteristics in the model). This strategy yielded 1,022 citizens who were asked to control themselves by the police. Reading the narratives we were able to apply our coding scheme to 939 cases and generate usable data. In the remainder of the cases the narratives were of insufficient detail to determine whether a compliance request occurred. Despite the loss of 83 cases, usable data were generated from nearly 92 percent of the original sample of 1,022. Dependent and independent measures for the phase I analysis are presented in Table 5.1.[1]

Table 5.1 Descriptive Statistics for Phase I Variables

	Min.	Max.	Mean	S.D.
Dependent Variable				
Citizen Compliance (0=no, 1=yes)	0	1	0.69	0.46
Independent Variables				
Police Entry	1	6	2.30	0.89
Indicators of Procedural Justice				
Citizen Entry (Rectitude) (0=no, 1=yes)	0	1	0.01	0.09
Citizen Entry (Morality) (0=no, 1=yes)	0	1	0.02	0.15
Police Respect Citizen (0=no, 1=yes)	0	1	0.17	0.38
Police Disrespect Citizen (0=no, 1=yes)	0	1	0.09	0.29
Citizen has Voice (0=no, 1=yes)	0	1	0.37	0.48
Citizen's Voice Terminated (0=no, 1=yes)	0	1	0.04	0.21
Police Seek Information: Identity (0=no, 1=yes)	0	1	0.51	0.50
Police Seek Information: Situation (0=no, 1=yes)	0	1	0.66	0.47
Police Seek Information: Solution (0=no, 1=yes)	0	1	0.05	0.21
Police Indicate Bias (0=no, 1=yes)	0	1	0.05	0.22
Police Indicate Leniency (0=no, 1=yes)	0	1	0.12	0.33
Police Indicate Independence (0=no, 1=yes)	0	1	0.05	0.22
Police have Probable Cause (0=no, 1=yes)	0	1	0.56	0.50
Indicators of Police Coercion				
Police Mention Arrest (0=no, 1=yes)	0	1	0.20	0.40
Police Make Suggestion (0=no, 1=yes)	0	1	0.07	0.26
Police Command (0=no, 1=yes)	0	1	0.20	0.40
Police Threaten (0=no, 1=yes)	0	1	0.12	0.32
Citizen Handcuffed (0=no, 1=yes)	0	1	0.06	0.24
Citizen Searched (0=no, 1=yes)	0	1	0.11	0.31
Physical Force v Citizen (0=no, 1=yes)	0	1	0.04	0.19
Gender Dyad	1	3	1.90	0.57
Citizen Arrested (0=no, 1=yes)	0	1	0.03	0.16
Citizen Cited (0=no, 1=yes)	0	1	0.06	0.24

	Min.	Max.	Mean	S.D.
Citizen has Weapon (0=no, 1=yes)	0	1	0.04	0.19
Number of Police Present (square root)	0	3.46	0.26	0.51
Number of Citizens Present (square root)	0	9.95	1.09	1.10
Police Command Self Control (0=no, 1=yes)	0	1	0.61	0.49
Third Party Influences on Target Citizens				
3rd Party Positive Verbalization (0=no, 1=yes)	0	1	0.04	0.19
3rd Party Negative Verbalization (0=no, 1=yes)	0	1	0.03	0.17
3rd Party Rebellion (0=no, 1=yes)	0	1	0.10	0.29
3rd Party Compliant (0=no, 1=yes)	0	1	0.23	0.42
Relative is Adversary (0=no, 1=yes)	0	1	0.16	0.36
Adversary Present (0=no, 1=yes)	0	1	0.32	0.47
Relative Present (0=no, 1=yes)	0	1	0.25	0.43
Key Citizen and Officer Characteristics				
Indicators of Irrationality	0	3	0.58	0.72
Citizen Age	1	8	5.14	1.47
Officer Minority (0=no, 1=yes)	0	1	0.20	0.40
Citizen Minority (0=no, 1=yes)	0	1	0.62	0.49
Citizen Low Income (0=no, 1=yes)	0	1	0.61	0.49

DEPENDENT VARIABLE

Our dependent variable is a binary measure of citizen compliance with the first request for self-control during the police-citizen encounter. Those citizens who comply on scene (212, or 23 percent of the sample) or promise to comply (439, or 47 percent) with the police request are considered compliant and are coded as one. Citizens who ignore the police request (137, or 15 percent) or refuse to obey (151, or 16 percent) are considered noncompliant and are coded as zero. For the sample 69 percent of the citizens were compliant in phase I of the encounter.

INDEPENDENT VARIABLES

Descriptive measures are presented in table 5.1 and will be used for modeling target compliance with requests for self-control. Unless noted as a measure taken from the original POPN coded data, each of these measures was hand coded from the narratives written by observers as outlined in chapter four. Variables that have multiple categories are presented in detail to further address the distribution of those variables. We discuss our independent measures in five broad categories. First, we address the entry tactics that police adopted during these encounters. Second, we examine the tactics police may use in encounters that would be considered fair or unfair procedures in accordance with our prior theoretical arguments. Third, we measure the various forms of coercive behavior that police use in encounters with citizens and capture several other important variables that may influence the coercive power of target and requestor. Fourth, we discuss the variables that capture third-party influence on citizens' on scene behavior. Finally, we discuss our measures of key citizen and officer characteristics that may influence the likelihood of compliance.

Entry

Police entry tactics are measured by a six-category variable that ranges from passive action, or presence only, to using physical force or arresting the target citizen (1=passive 2=ask questions, 3=issue commands, 4=issue threat, 5=physical force, 6=arrested citizen). Our assumption is that these tactics range from the least coercive (presence only) to the most coercive (legal custody) and represent an ordinal scale of coercive police action. The mean of the variable is 2.30, and the modal category is asking questions. In 560 cases, or about 60 percent of the encounters, the police asked a question on entry. Police issued commands upon entry in 228 encounters or 24 percent of the encounters. Passive behavior by police was the next most common entry tactic, occurring in 101 cases or nearly eleven percent of the sample. Physical force on entry by the police was observed in 28 cases or three percent of the encounters. Arresting the citizen on entry occurred in 13 cases and issuing a threat to citizens occurred in 9 cases, each amounting to about one percent of the sample. That distribution of entry tactics is heavily weighted towards asking questions and issuing commands is not surprising given the micro-analysis of police-citizen interaction performed by Sykes and Brent (1980). Asking questions and establishing verbal control of the police-citizen interaction are a primary action of police according to their analysis as well as the ethnographic work of Muir (1977).

Indicators of Procedural Justice

Thirteen indicators of procedural justice were coded from the narrative data. Unless otherwise noted, the variables were coded one if the condition was present and zero if the condition was not present. The first two variables indicate whether the citizens' believed the police to be lacking in authority at the scene (morality) or whether police presence was considered to be appropriate (rectitude) by the target. These two indicators were measured by verbal comments from the target prior to any police action. Neither negative regard for police, which occurred 22 times in the sample, nor positive comment toward the police, which occurred 8 times, was frequently observed. Both indicators appeared in approximately one percent of the cases, and raise the concern of quasi-complete separation with respect to the logistic model (Menard, 1995).

Indicators of respectful and disrespectful treatment of the target by police were coded prior to the request for compliance. In seventeen percent of the cases the police were respectful of the target and in nine percent of the cases police displayed disrespect towards the target. These categories are not exclusive. In 17 cases, or about two percent of the sample, police were both disrespectful and respectful of the target prior to requesting self-control.

Voice effects were measured using two variables. The first captured whether the citizen had an opportunity to tell the police his side of the story, which occurred in 37 percent of the cases in our sample. The second captured whether the police terminated the citizen's voice by asking him to be quiet or shut up. That occurred in four percent of the cases in the sample.

Three variables measured police information seeking on the scene, which should generate a sense of police making an informed decision. We coded whether police asked the citizen for identifying information, an explanation of the presenting situation, and how the police might best handle the situation. In our sample we found these variables to be present in 51 percent, 66 percent, and five percent of the cases, respectively. In only 22 percent of the cases did the police ask for none of these types of information and in 42 percent they asked for two or more types of information.

Three other measures capture whether the police made indications to the citizen about how they were making decisions, and whether those decisions were "quality" decisions in the context of the encounter. First, we measured whether the police indicated that their decision was biased, or based on the preferences of another citizen at the scene. Evidence of biased decision-making was present in five percent of the sample. Second, we measured whether the police indicated that the solution was lenient when compared with what the police could potentially do with the target citizen. In twelve percent of the sample cases police indicated to citizens that they were making a lenient decision with respect to the target citizen. We also measured whether the police indicated that their decision was rooted in law, an arguably independent standard. In five percent of the sample cases the police overtly rooted their decisions in legal code.

Whether police had probable cause to stop the citizen, which would influence the legitimacy of their presence at the scene, was measured as being present when the evidence level rises to two or more points from the coding scheme presented in chapter four. The presence of probable cause is expected to be positively related to the likelihood of compliance. The police had probable cause prior to the request for self-control in 56 percent of the encounters in our sample.

Coercion

Nine police tactics are measured using dummy variables (1=tactic used 0=tactic not used) and include mentioning arrest, making a suggestion, issuing commands, issuing threats, handcuffing, searching, physical force, arresting, and citing the target citizen. Prior to requesting self-control the police mentioned arrest in twenty percent of the encounters, made a suggestion in seven percent, issued a command in twenty percent, and threatened citizens in twelve percent. The police handcuffed the target in six percent of the cases and searched them in eleven percent of the cases. Finally, the police arrested the citizen prior to requesting self-control in three percent of the cases, and cited the citizen in six percent of the cases.

Gender dyad is a variable measuring the gender relationship between the target and the requestor (1=female target/male requestor, 2=target/requestor same gender, 3=male target/female requestor). The variable transforms the conceptualization of gender, as a representation of coercive balance of power, as suggest by Katz (1988). This was computed from the coded data collected by the observers regarding the gender of the citizen and surveys conducted by POPN researchers that coded the gender of the observed officer. The mean level of variable is 1.90, and the modal category is target and requestor share the same gender. In 22 percent of the cases female targets are paired with male police officers and in twelve percent of the cases male citizens are paired with female police officers. We use the square root transformation of the number of officers on scene to measure the number of officers (besides the observed officer) on scene at the beginning of the encounter, because of skewness in the data. Untransformed this variable ranges from zero to twelve, but the transformed variable ranges from zero to 3.46 with standard deviation of .51. In 78 percent of the cases there were no other officers on scene and the mean number of other officers on scene was .36. Finally, we use a square root transformation of the number of citizens (besides the target) who are on scene at the beginning of the encounter. The untransformed variable ranges from zero to 99, with 73 percent of the cases indicating two or fewer citizens on scene. To address the distribution the variable was transformed, which resulted in a mean level of 1.11 and a range from zero to seven. Both untransformed variables, the number of police and the number of citizens on scene at the beginning of the encounter, were taken from the data coded by the observers rather than coded from narratives.

Two other indicators of coercive power during the target-requestor interaction were measured prior to the conclusion of phase I. First, we coded a dummy variable to capture whether the citizen had a weapon during phase I of the encounter. Four percent of the sample cases involved citizens who possessed weapons. Second, we coded the level of the self-control request as being a command or threat by the police. In 61 percent of the sample cases the police commanded or threatened the citizen to engage in self-control.

Third Party Influences

Milgram's work in social psychology indicates the importance of allies, colleagues, or models in guiding one's behavior, especially with regard to obedience to authority figures. Two hypotheses can be drawn from that work, which are germane to the police-citizen encounter. First, if citizens are in the presence of a non-cooperative citizen, then they would be more likely to be disobedient. Conversely one would expect that if target citizens are in the presence of a cooperative third party then they will be more likely to comply. Another consideration of third party influence is whether the target citizen is dealing with someone that could be considered an adversary at the scene and whether the target has a pre-existing relationship with an adversary or non-adversary at the scene.

A pair of dummy variables is included that capture whether a third party made positive or negative remarks about the police prior to the request for self control in phase I. In four percent of the cases a third party made a positive comment and in three percent of the cases a third party made a negative comment. We also measure two variables that capture third party responses to police requests for self-control. The first assesses whether there was a rebellious person on scene prior to the request to the target citizen. In ten percent of the sample cases a rebellious citizen was present. The second variable captures whether a compliant citizen was present at the scene, which occurred in 23 percent of the observed cases. In 21 instances third parties that were compliant and noncompliant were in the presence of the target citizen prior to the request for self-control.

Three variables capture the presence of relatives and adversaries at the scene. First we measure whether there was a adversary present, which occurred in 32 percent of the cases. Second, we measure whether there was a relative present, which occurred in 25 percent of the cases. Finally, we measured whether there was a relative that was an adversary on the scene prior to the request for self control, which occurred in sixteen percent of the sample cases.

Key Citizen Characteristics

Five citizen and officer characteristics were measured to model target compliance with requests for self-control in this sample. Each of these measures was compiled from the observational data coded by the observers. First we measure the number of irrational elements the target displayed, including whether the citizen appeared drunk, mentally ill, or under the influence of heightened emotions. An ordinal variable was constructed by summing the number of irrational factors influencing the citizen and ranges from zero to three. That measure had a mean of .58 and 55 percent of the target citizens in the sample had no irrational influences affecting their behavior. Of those with one or more factors influencing their behavior 45 (4.8 percent) had evidence of mental illness, 172 (18.3 percent) had behavioral effects of alcohol or drugs, and 324 (34.5 percent) had evidence of strong emotions or anger as an irrational element in this index.

The second measure of individual characteristics is the citizen's age, which is an eight category variable coded by trained observers at the time of the encounter. This variable subdivides chronological age into broad categories (1=5 and under; 2=6-12 years; 3=13-17; 4=18-20; 5=21-29; 6=30-44; 7=45-59; 8=60 and above), and has a mean of 5.14. The modal age range represents adults 30 to 44, comprising 36 percent of the sample. Categories three through five, which range from 13 to 29 years old represent 15 percent, 10 percent, and 22 percent of the target citizens in the sample, respectively. Very young targets under 13, and older targets over 45 are limited to less than ten percent of the sample.

Minority status of the observed officer is measured by a dummy variable and indicates that twenty percent of the target sample encounters involved minority officers. Similarly, a dummy variable is used to measure whether the target had minority status. This sample of citizens asked to control their behaviors is composed of 62 percent minority target citizens. A measure of income coded by observers who assessed the citizens' level of wealth indicated whether citizens appeared to be in chronic poverty, lower class, or middle class, or upper class. We collapsed these categories into a dummy variable with chronic poverty and lower income citizens as low income (1) and middle and upper class citizens as the reference (0) category. Of the sample cases 61 percent were coded as low income.

MODELING REQUESTS FOR SELF-CONTROL

Since the dependent variable is binary we use logistic regression models to estimate models of target compliance (Long 1997; Menard

1995). To assess the individual contributions of the domains of variables we have outlined above, we opt to step the variables into a logistic model to determine where significant explanatory power exists. To do this we will examine measures of fit and some pseudo-measures of explanatory power that must be judiciously interpreted (Long 1997). Pseudo-R^2 measures do not have the properties of the R^2 that is typically associated with OLS regression; thus, our inference about explanatory power is much weaker. We will rely most heavily on model fit statistics to offer some insight into the relative utility of the domains for explaining why citizens comply with police requests.

Tables 5.2a and 5.2b contains the results of four logistic regression models predicting cooperation with police requests for self control during phase I (n.b., that model I, featuring entry tactics, is not presented in tables but instead explained in the text). We entered the domains separately to assess how well each set of variables fared in predicting whether citizens would comply with the request for self-control. These models represent the explanatory utility for each of the domains, as isolated variable sets, and as such we will limit our interpretation to the model fit, rather than the interpretation of individual coefficients. In a sense this provides an estimate of how much explanatory power each domain possesses in explaining citizen compliance. In each model the x^2 statistic indicates that the domains have at least one predictor that is not equal to zero. The pseudo-R^2 measures suggest that the procedural justice domain, third party domain, and officer and citizen characteristics provide moderate explanatory power with respect to citizen compliance.

As a next step, we enter each domain into the model to determine what indicators from each domain are the most powerful determinants of citizen compliance. The domains were stepped into the equation using a mixture of event timing and theoretical importance. We entered the following blocks of variables, in this order, into our model: Entry tactics, procedural justice indicators, indicators of coercion, third party influences, and citizen and officer characteristics. To test the significance of each block entered into the model we use a likelihood ratio chi-square test, which measures whether the block introduces significant improvement over the model omitting that block (Long, 1997: 94-96). The model chi-square is also reported to measure whether the model is a better than chance fit to the data. Results are presented in tables 5.3a and 5.3b.

Table 5.2a Logistic Models for Each Domain

	Model II			Model III		
	B	**S.E.**	**Exp(B)**	**B**	**S.E.**	**Exp(B)**
Constant	0.05	0.16		0.99*	0.28	
Police Entry						
Procedural Justice						
Citizen Entry (Rectitude)	5.58	7.71	266.07			
Citizen Entry (Morality)	-0.42	0.48	0.66			
Police Respect Citizen	0.60*	0.24	1.82			
Police Disrespect Citizen	-0.66*	0.25	0.52			
Citizen has Voice	0.03	0.17	1.03			
Citizen's Voice Terminated	-1.01*	0.35	0.37			
Police Seek Information : Identity	0.64*	0.16	1.90			
Police Seek Information : Situation	0.63*	0.16	1.87			
Police Seek Information : Solution	0.30	0.39	1.35			
Police Indicate Bias	-0.17	0.34	0.84			
Police Indicate Leniency	1.88*	0.44	6.58			
Police Indicate Independence	0.11	0.34	1.11			
Police have Probable Cause	-0.08	0.16	0.92			
Police Coercion						
Police Mention Arrest				0.76*	0.22	2.14
Police Make Suggestion				0.68*	0.34	1.97
Police Command				0.06	0.19	1.06
Police Threaten				0.10	0.27	1.10
Citizen Handcuffed				-0.50	0.36	0.61
Citizen Searched				0.84*	0.29	2.31
Physical Force v Citizen				-0.67*	0.40	0.51
Gender Dyad				-0.01	0.13	0.99
Citizen Arrested				-1.28*	0.50	0.28
Citizen Cited				0.54	0.37	1.72
Citizen has Weapon				0.16	0.42	1.18
Number of Police Present (sqrt)				-0.26*	0.15	0.77
Number of Citizens Present (sqrt)				-0.16*	0.07	0.86
Police Command Self Control				-0.22	0.16	0.80
Model X^2	131.02*	13 df		59.44*	14 df	
Nagelkerke R^2	.18			.09		

*$p<.05$, one-tailed test

Table 5.2b Logistic Models for Each Domain

	Model IV			Model V		
	B	**S.E.**	**Exp(B)**	**B**	**S.E.**	**Exp(B)**
Constant	0.93*	0.10		0.69*	0.30	
Third Party Influences						
3rd Party Positive Verbalization	-0.01	0.38	0.99			
3rd Party Negative Verbalization	0.20	0.44	1.22			
3rd Party Rebellion	-1.22*	0.25	0.29			
3rd Party Compliant	1.32*	0.23	3.74			
Relative is Adversary	0.03	0.32	1.03			
Adversary Present	-0.67*	0.21	0.51			
Relative Present	0.04	0.27	1.04			
Key Citizen/Officer Characteristics						
Indicators of Irrationality				-0.97*	0.11	0.38
Citizen Age				0.20*	0.05	1.22
Officer Minority				-0.31*	0.18	0.73
Citizen Minority				-0.10	0.16	0.90
Citizen Low Income				-0.17	0.16	0.84
Model X^2	90.38*	7df		99.11*	5 df	
Nagelkerke R^2	.13			.14		

*$p<.05$, one-tailed test

The variable measuring entry tactics was entered in model I (not shown) since it captures the first actions of the police on scene. The model chi-square test ($x^2=17.02$, 1 d.f.) indicates that the model is a significant improvement over chance. Police entry tactics are significant and negatively related to citizen compliance, indicating that as police are more forceful on entry, citizens are less likely to cooperate when asked for self-control. One could interpret a finding as an indication that police attend to factors on entry that relate to the likelihood of compliance and enter at higher levels of coercion in situations where compliance is less likely. Our analysis cannot verify or falsify that hypothesis.

Table 5.3a Nested Logistic Models II – III

	Model II			Model III		
	B	**S.E.**	**Exp(B)**	**B**	**S.E.**	**Exp(B)**
Constant	0.59*	0.28		0.38	0.42	
Police Entry	-0.21*	0.09	0.81	-0.16	0.10	0.85
Procedural Justice						
Citizen Entry (Rectitude)	5.50	7.70	243.87	5.84	7.70	342.65
Citizen Entry (Morality)	-0.58	0.49	0.56	-0.61	0.50	0.54
Police Respect Citizen	0.64*	0.24	1.90	0.62*	0.25	1.86
Police Disrespect Citizen	-0.59*	0.26	0.55	-0.66*	0.27	0.52
Citizen has Voice	-0.03	0.17	0.97	0.04	0.18	1.04
Citizen's Voice Terminated	-0.97*	0.35	0.38	-1.01*	0.37	0.36
Police Seek Information : Identity	0.62*	0.16	1.85	0.64*	0.17	1.89
Police Seek Information : Situation	0.56*	0.17	1.75	0.50*	0.17	1.66
Police Seek Information : Solution	0.21	0.39	1.23	0.22	0.39	1.25
Police Indicate Bias	-0.22	0.34	0.80	-0.14	0.35	0.87
Police Indicate Leniency	1.88*	0.44	6.52	1.77*	0.45	5.84
Police Indicate Independence	0.08	0.34	1.09	-0.02	0.35	0.98
Police have Probable Cause	-0.04	0.16	0.96	0.00	0.17	1.00
Police Coercion						
Police Mention Arrest				0.54*	0.25	1.71
Police Make Suggestion				0.58	0.36	1.79
Police Command				0.39*	0.21	1.48
Police Threaten				0.18	0.29	1.20
Citizen Handcuffed				-0.16	0.42	0.85
Citizen Searched				0.51	0.31	1.66
Physical Force v Citizen				-0.37	0.43	0.69
Gender Dyad				0.04	0.14	1.04
Citizen Arrested				-1.47*	0.55	0.23
Citizen Cited				-0.16	0.42	0.86
Citizen has Weapon				0.28	0.45	1.32
Number of Police Present (sqrt)				-0.18	0.16	0.84
Number of Citizens Present (sqrt)				-0.08	0.07	0.92
Police Command Self Control				-0.10	0.18	0.91
Model X²	136.75*	14 df		167.75*	28 df	
X² Improvement Statistic	119.73*	13 df		31.00*	14 df	
Nagelkerke R²	.19			.23		

* p < .05 one-tailed test

Table 5.3b Nested Logistic Models IV–V with Collinearity Diagnostics

	Model IV			Model V (Full Model)			Collinearity Diagostics
	B	**S.E.**	**Exp(B)**	**B**	**S.E.**	**Exp(B)**	**SQRT:VIF**
Constant	0.70	0.46		0.19	0.58		
Police Entry	-0.18	0.11	0.84	-0.12	0.11	0.89	1.23
Procedural Justice							
Citizen Entry (Rectitude)	5.76	7.59	316.37	5.39	7.55	218.51	1.04
Citizen Entry (Morality)	-0.67	0.52	0.51	-0.51	0.52	0.60	1.05
Police Respect Citizen	0.63*	0.26	1.87	0.63*	0.27	1.88	1.07
Police Disrespect Citizen	-0.62*	0.28	0.54	-0.53*	0.29	0.59	1.09
Citizen has Voice	0.06	0.19	1.07	0.04	0.20	1.04	1.10
Voice Terminated	-0.73*	0.39	0.48	-0.70*	0.41	0.50	1.06
Information: Identity	0.31	0.19	1.36	0.21	0.20	1.23	1.22
Information: Situation	0.73*	0.19	2.08	0.74*	0.20	2.09	1.14
Information: Solution	0.34	0.42	1.41	0.39	0.43	1.48	1.06
Indicate Bias	0.00	0.37	1.00	-0.25	0.38	0.78	1.05
Indicate Leniency	1.83*	0.46	6.20	1.88*	0.48	6.57	1.11
Indicate Independence	-0.11	0.38	0.90	-0.16	0.38	0.86	1.05
Probable Cause	-0.17	0.18	0.85	-0.17	0.19	0.85	1.13
Police Coercion							
Police Mention Arrest	0.38	0.26	1.46	0.39	0.27	1.48	1.19
Police Make Suggestion	0.58	0.37	1.78	0.57	0.39	1.78	1.06
Police Command	0.37*	0.22	1.45	0.34	0.22	1.40	1.07
Police Threaten	0.09	0.30	1.10	0.01	0.31	1.01	1.16
Citizen Handcuffed	0.09	0.44	1.10	-0.01	0.46	1.00	1.29
Citizen Searched	0.24	0.33	1.27	0.23	0.33	1.26	1.11
Physical Force v Citizen	-0.43	0.44	0.65	-0.04	0.45	0.97	1.10
Gender Dyad	0.02	0.14	1.03	-0.02	0.15	0.98	1.04
Citizen Arrested	-1.37*	0.57	0.25	-1.22*	0.58	0.30	1.17
Citizen Cited	-0.03	0.43	0.97	-0.26	0.43	0.77	1.08
Citizen has Weapon	0.42	0.44	1.53	0.40	0.45	1.49	1.05
Police Present (sqrt)	-0.18	0.17	0.84	-0.17	0.17	0.84	1.09
Citizens Present (sqrt)	-0.10	0.08	0.90	-0.06	0.08	0.95	1.17
Command Self Control	-0.14	0.19	0.87	-0.07	0.20	0.93	1.16

	Model IV			Model V (Full Model)			Collinearity Diagostics
	B	**S.E.**	**Exp(B)**	**B**	**S.E.**	**Exp(B)**	**SQRT:VIF**
Third Party Influences							
Positive Verbalization	-0.07	0.42	0.93	0.03	0.44	1.03	1.06
Negative Verbalization	0.43	0.52	1.53	0.48	0.52	1.61	1.06
Rebellion	-1.16*	0.28	0.31	-1.14*	0.29	0.32	1.07
Compliant	1.38*	0.25	3.99	1.27*	0.26	3.57	1.11
Relative is Adversary	0.11	0.35	1.12	0.11	0.36	1.11	1.67
Adversary Present	-0.56*	0.25	0.57	-0.32	0.26	0.73	1.51
Relative Present	-0.15	0.30	0.86	-0.02	0.31	0.98	1.64
Key Citizen/Officer Characteristics							
Indicators of Irrationality				-0.70*	0.13	0.50	1.16
Citizen Age				0.16*	0.06	1.18	1.12
Officer Minority				-0.23	0.21	0.80	1.04
Citizen Minority				-0.10	0.18	0.91	1.05
Citizen Low Income				0.06	0.18	1.06	1.07
Model X^2	232.68* 35 df			267.23* 40 df			
X^2 Improvement Statistic	64.93* 7 df			34.55* 5 df			
Nagelkerke R^2	.31			.35			

*p < .05 one-tailed test

Thirteen indicators of procedural justice are entered on the next step in model II. The chi-square test indicates that the model fit is better than chance (x^2=136.75, 14 d.f.), and the likelihood ratio test statistic indicates that the block of procedural justice indicators is also significant (x^2=119.73, 13 d.f.). Entry tactics remain significant and are negatively related to citizen compliance. In addition, police disrespect, police respect, termination of citizen voice, seeking information about identity and the situation, and police indicating leniency are all significant predictors of citizen compliance with requests for self-control and are in the expected directions predicted from our theory.

Model III includes fourteen indicators of coercion, and the model chi-square is significant (x^2=167.75, 28 d.f.). The likelihood ratio test chi-square statistic is also significant (x^2=31.00, 14 d.f.), indicating that, as a block, the indicators of coercion do offer a significant improvement over model II in predicting whether citizens comply with requests for self control. Police entry tactics are not significantly different from zero in model III, but the procedural justice indicators maintained their signs and significance, indicating stability in that block. Of the variables in the coercion domain three were significant predictors of citizen compliance. Police mentioning arrests and issuing commands were, consonant with our theory, positive predictors of compliance. Conversely, once citizens were arrested, they were less likely to comply with the police request for self-control. This finding, though not what we would predict from social-interactionist theory, comports with the cautionary notes offered by Mastrofski, Snipes, and Supina (1996) in their initial examination of citizen compliance. Arrest may change the landscape of police-citizen interaction from an adversarial relationship to a custodial relationship, which may impact the likelihood of target cooperation and the utility of our overall theoretical framework.

Model IV includes seven indicators of third party influence as a block in the larger model. Both the model chi-square (x^2=232.68, 35 d.f.) and the likelihood ratio statistic associated with the improvement achieved by including the block (x^2=64.93, 7 d.f.) are significant. The coefficients from model III were stable in sign and significance, except for police seeking information of the target's identity and police mentioning arrest, which were non-significant in model IV. In terms of the third party influences on the likelihood of citizen compliance with requests for self control, three indicators were significant and in the expected directions. Third party rebellion and the presence of an adversary at the scene both depressed the likelihood of citizen compliance significantly. The presence of a compliant citizen, conversely, significantly increased the likelihood of citizen compliance with police requests for self control.

Five indicators of officer and citizen characteristics were added in model V. The model chi-square (x^2=267.23, 40 d.f.) and the likelihood ratio test chi-square (x^2=34.55, 5 d.f.) were both significant for this model. This indicates that the model is a better than chance predictor of citizen compliance and that the citizen characteristics are better than chance predictors of compliance. Two significant predictors from model IV are non-significant in the full model, including police use of commands and the presence of an adversary. Of the key citizen and officer characteristics, citizen irrationality is negatively associated with compliance, as predicted by theory. Also consonant with our theory is the significant and positive influence of age on the likelihood of citizen compliance.

The full model has 40 predictors, but offers only ten indicators that can be distinguished from zero with respect to predicting the likelihood of compliance with police requests for self-control. As a block, the domain of procedural justice indicators produced five of those predictors. Holding all else constant, citizens who receive respectful treatment from authorities are almost twice as likely to comply, and those receiving disrespectful treatment are nearly twice as likely to rebel. If the citizen's voice is terminated by the police they are more than twice as likely to rebel against the police request for self-control. If the police demonstrate their commitment to making an informed decision by seeking information about the presenting situation, citizens are more than twice as likely to comply with the phase I request for self-control. Finally, holding all else constant, when police inform the target citizen that they are acting in a lenient fashion, the citizens are six and a half times more likely to comply with the self-control request.

In terms of coercion, only arrest has an impact on the likelihood of citizen compliance that could be distinguished from zero.[2] Citizens who are arrested are three times less likely to comply, holding all else constant, when compared to those targets who were not arrested prior to the phase I request. As noted above, this represents an affirmation of the cautionary note Mastrofski, Snipes, and Supina (1996) mentioned in their seminal work on compliance. Since the direction of the arrest coefficient is the opposite of our theorized impact, we can only surmise that arrest transforms the police-target relationship from adversarial in nature to custodial. Accompanying the new custodial role of the police officer is a much reduced arsenal of coercive actions and procedurally just actions, since a verdict has, arguably, been rendered in the case of the target. Such speculation requires further investigation beyond the scope of this research.

Third party responses to police requests for compliance yield two significant predictors of target compliance. These findings comport with the Milgram's commentary on behavioral modeling in the face of authority. Targets are 3.5 times more likely to obey the police, holding all else constant, when there is a third party displaying obedience to that authority. Conversely, when a third party fails to display compliance upon request to the police, the citizen is slightly more than three times less likely to comply with the police request for self-control.

Two citizen characteristics are significant predictors of compliance with police requests for self-control in phase I. For every unit increase in the number of irrational elements affecting a citizen, the citizen becomes two times less likely to comply with the police request. For every one unit increase in the age variable, citizens are 1.18 times more likely to comply with the police request for self-control.

Overall, significant predictors in the full model maintained relative stability as domains were added. One variable raising concern about model fit across all models is positive comments upon citizen entry (more specifically, those cases where the target citizen mentioned the rectitude of police presence prior to any substantive police action), which has an inflated beta of 5.39 (consistent from the theory's prediction), a standard error of 7.55, and an odds ratio of 218.51. This indicates that, though not statistically significant, citizens who make positive comments about the police are 218 times more likely to comply with their requests for self-control. All eight citizens vocalizing positive comments about the police, prior to any police action, were compliant. Our model thus suffers from complete separation on this variable, however, reestimating the model without this variable obtains nearly an identical result. We opt to present the more complete model, since our theoretical foundation required its inclusion.

Collinearity, or the intercorrelation of independent variables is a potential threat to the models built in table 5.3b. The square root of the variance inflation factor, is suggested by Fox (1991) as a useful screen for multi-collinearity. Menard (1995) suggests that collinearity diagnostics be estimated using OLS in the case of logistic regression. Variance inflation factors were calculated for the full logistic model with all domains entered. Fox (1991) suggests the square root of the variance inflation factor as a useful diagnostic for assessing models' problems with collinearity. Fox (1991) notes that independent variables' standard errors become a concern as this measure approaches the 2.29 threshold from the 1.67 threshold. In table 5.3b, only whether a relative was present or a relative was an adversary prior to requesting self-control approaches the lower boundary of concern. The full model, re-estimated excluding these two variables (they are interrelated with the presence of an adversary, as well as among themselves) remains consistent with the model presented in table 5.3b. Thus we are confident the logistic regression models of citizen compliance with requests for self-control are unthreatened by collinearity, despite the indication from the diagnostics that these two variables could be problematic.

Alternative Analytic Strategies

Our final model consists of forty predictors, which consume degrees of freedom for estimating our dependent variable. Although the model is not afflicted by collinearity it is ponderous in terms of the number of independent predictors of citizen's decision to exercise on scene self-control. Previously we mentioned that, if necessary, core concepts from social interactionist theory as well as procedural justice theory could be collapsed into indexes. The large number of predictors in our phase I model lead us to consider creating indexes of variables that are theoretically interrelated. Below we present arguments for creating five indexes that will reduce the model to 20 predictors of citizen compliance. This is defensible since we have argued a priori for such a tactic if the model was too cumbersome to estimate. Though that is not the case, since we have obtained estimates from our phase I models, we consider indexing our variables to be a worthwhile exercise in examining how these domains hold up under alternative operationalization. For example, one might be inclined to argue that the numerous indicators of officer coercion on scene might best be entered as an index of the most coercive officer action taken on scene. Below we present arguments for creating three procedural justice indexes, one index of police coercion, and one index of third party influence.

Among the procedural justice indices, the index of ethicality combines four police stimuli. To generate an index of ethicality we took the dummy variables representing police respect, police disrespect, whether the police gave the target an opportunity for voice, and police termination of voice using the following formula:

Index of Ethicality $=$

$$X_{respect} - X_{disrespect} + X_{opportunity\ for\ voice} - X_{termination\ of\ voice}.$$

Theoretically, respectfulness of behavior and allowing or terminating one's voice are closely related and are associated with the conduct expected of authorities. Thus we argue that we are justified in making a composite index of the four indicator variables. This index is correlated with respect (r=.60), disrespect (r=-.40), opportunity for voice (r=.69), and termination of voice (r=-.30) in the direction we would anticipate.

A second index of procedurally just actions, which we term the index of information seeking, combines three variables; whether police seek information about the target's identity, the presenting situation, or how to resolve the presenting situation. To generate this index we summed the three indicators of information seeking in the following fashion:

Index of Information Seeking =

$$x_{\text{info on identity}} + x_{\text{info on situation}} + x_{\text{info on resolution}}.$$

In our theoretical justification for including police directed information seeking we argue for the inclusion of such indicators based on their demonstration that police are attempting to make a fair understanding of the presenting situation. The index is correlated with seeking information on identity (r=.75), seeking information on the situation (r=.77), and seeking information about the appropriate solution to the situation (r=.29), consistent with our expectation that this formula generates a meaningful summary of police actions during the initial phase of the police-citizen encounters.

The final index of procedural justice indicators created was the index of the quality of decision-making. For this index we summed the indicators for bias, independence, and leniency in the following formula:

Index of Decision-making quality = $x_{\text{leniency}} - x_{\text{bias}} + x_{\text{independence}}.$

Of the three indices, this arguably represents how decision-making of the authorities is presented to the citizen. Biased decisions rooted in the concerns of adversaries will likely generate a negative sense of fairness and independent decision-making is likely to generate the opposite. Leniency is included in this composite since, by definition, it indicates that the police held the citizen's behavior against a standard and chose to impose a solution below the most serious on that continuum. One should note the solution does not have to be an arrest, but can merely be, for example, not telling a juvenile's parents about the situation if the juvenile engages in self-control. Like independence it reflects an authority making a decision that is tailored to the situation and is likely to generate a sense that the decision was arrived at fairly. The index of decision-making quality is correlated with the mention of leniency (r=.70), indication of independence (r=.47), and the indication of a biased decision (r=-.52) in a manner that is consistent with our expectations. A valid concern for the inclusion of leniency in this construct is whether it is a substantive outcome, rather than a procedural act. We argue that the mention of leniency of the authority's decision is procedural, inasmuch as that allows the target to understand how a decision was reached.

Our index of police coercion was generated by coding an ordinal variable that represents the most coercive tactic that police made during phase I of the encounter. To construct an index of coercive police actions we chose to code the highest level of coercion present prior to the request for self-control, net of the entry tactics. This ordinal variable captures whether the police used no action (0), suggestions (1), commands (2), threats (3), handcuffing, searching, or physical contact/force (4), arrest or cite (5) as the highest action. Categories four and five are consistent with our coding of entry tactics except that we had to include citations in category five as a legal action, since there were so few. Reversing these two categories obtains nearly the same effects in the models presented below, for this ordinal index of coercion.

To capture third party influences on targets' compliance we constructed an index using third party negative and positive verbalization, third party compliance and rebellion, and the presence of an adversary. From a theoretical standpoint, the positive models by third parties (compliant behavior, positive remarks regarding police) and negative models (rebelling behavior, or negative remarks) represent opposite influences in the universe of third party actions. This index was constructed using the following formula:

$$\text{Index of 3}^{rd}\text{ Party} = x_{\text{positive verbal}} - x_{\text{negative verbal}} + x_{\text{compliant}} - x_{\text{rebels}}.$$

The index is correlated with third party positive verbalizations (r=.34), third party negative verbalizations (r=-.43), third party compliance (r=.70), and third party rebellion (r=-.56) in a manner consistent with our expectations. The signs and magnitudes of the correlations give weight to the index representing a composite measure of third party influences within this sample of police-citizen encounters.

The distributions of the indexes are presented in table 5.4. The index of ethicality has a range from negative two to positive two, and a mean of .41. The modal category for the index is zero, with 53 percent of the sample cases. The index of information seeking ranges from zero to three, with a mean level of 1.21. The modal category of information seeking elements is two with 40 percent of the cases falling in that category. The decision-making index ranges from negative one to one, with a mean of .13. The modal category of the index is zero, with nearly 79 percent of the cases falling in that category. The composite variable representing the highest level of coercion ranges from zero to five, with a mean level of 2.07. The modal category of coercive action is issuing commands, which was the most coercive in 42 percent of the sample cases. Finally, the index of third party influences ranged from negative two to positive two with a mean level of .14. The modal category in this variable is zero, which is present in 68 percent of the cases.

Table 5.4 Distribution of Indexes in Phase I (n=939)

Index	Min.	Max.	Mean	S.D.
Ethicality	-2	2	0.41	0.73
Information Seeking	0	3	1.21	0.80
Decision-Making	-1	1	0.13	0.44
Coercion	0	5	2.07	1.55
Third Party Influences	-2	2	0.14	0.60

In tables 5.5 and 5.6 we develop a similar model building scheme, beginning with entry tactics, procedural justice, coercion, third party influences, and generating the full model by entering the citizen and officer characteristics block. Rather than address each step in detail we will merely assess the fit at each step. Entry tactics is a significant improvement over chance (x^2=17.71, 1 d.f.), and identical to the model presented previously. Beginning, then, with the procedural justice domain we find those predictors as a block generate a statistically significant likelihood ratio test chi-square (x^2=89.58, 6 d.f.) indicating significant model improvement. The block of coercive power indicators, conversely, generates a non-significant likelihood ratio test chi-square (x^2=12.21, 6 d.f.), indicating that this block of predictors does not significantly enhance the predictive power of the model. The inclusion of third party influences in model IV generates a statistically significant likelihood ratio test chi-square (x^2=54.27, 4 d.f.), indicating that this block of predictors adds significantly to the explanation of citizens' decision to comply. Finally, the addition of key citizen and officer characteristics generates a significant likelihood statistic (x^2=43.25, 5 d.f.), indicating that, as a block, the impact of at least one predictor is different from zero.

Table 5.5 Index Substitution

	Model II			Model III		
	B	**S.E.**	**Exp(B)**	**B**	**S.E.**	**Exp(B)**
Constant	0.43	0.26	1.53	0.40	0.37	1.50
Police Entry	-0.19*	0.08	0.83	-0.16*	0.09	0.85
Procedural Justice Indicators						
Citizen Entry (Rectitude)	5.46	7.66	235.90	5.63	7.66	279.00
Citizen Entry (Morality)	-0.73	0.46	0.48	-0.74	0.47	0.48
Index of Ethicality	0.39*	0.11	1.47	0.39*	0.11	1.48
Index of Information Seeking	0.55*	0.10	1.73	0.52*	0.10	1.68
Index of Decision-Making	0.71*	0.19	2.04	0.69*	0.20	2.00
Probable Cause	0.03	0.16	1.03	-0.01	0.16	0.99
Indicators of Police Coercion						
Police Mention Arrest				0.56*	0.22	1.75
Index of Police Coercion				-0.04	0.06	0.97
Gender Dyad				0.08	0.13	1.08
Citizen has Weapon				0.44	0.43	1.55
Police Present (square root)				-0.28*	0.15	0.76
Citizens Present (square root)				-0.08	0.07	0.92
Model X^2	106.61*	7 df		118.82*	13 df	
X^2 Improvement Statistic	89.58*	6 df		12.21	6 df	
Nagelkerke R^2	.15			.17		

*p < .05, one-tailed

Table 5.6 Index Substitution

	Model IV			Model V		
	B	**S.E.**	**Exp(B)**	**B**	**S.E.**	**Exp(B)**
Constant	0.83*	0.41	2.30	0.23	0.53	1.26
Police Entry	-0.16*	0.10	0.85	-0.09	0.10	0.92
Procedural Justice Indicators						
Citizen Entry (Rectitude)	5.32	7.69	204.43	5.04	7.66	154.90
Citizen Entry (Morality)	-0.70	0.49	0.50	-0.46	0.51	0.63
Index of Ethicality	0.40*	0.12	1.49	0.37*	0.12	1.45
Index of Information Seeking	0.50*	0.11	1.64	0.45*	0.11	1.57
Index of Decision-Making	0.62*	0.20	1.86	0.64*	0.21	1.89
Probable Cause	-0.17	0.17	0.84	-0.18	0.18	0.83
Indicators of Police Coercion						
Police Mention Arrest	0.42*	0.23	1.52	0.46*	0.23	1.58
Index of Police Coercion	-0.06	0.06	0.95	-0.04	0.06	0.96
Gender Dyad	0.03	0.14	1.03	-0.01	0.14	0.99
Citizen has Weapon	0.62	0.43	1.86	0.55	0.44	1.73
Police Present (sqrt)	-0.27*	0.16	0.76	-0.24	0.16	0.78
Citizens Present (sqrt)	-0.07	0.07	0.93	-0.03	0.08	0.97
Third Party Influences						
Third Party Index	0.80*	0.14	2.23	0.75*	0.15	2.12
Relative is Adversary	0.00	0.33	1.00	0.01	0.34	1.01
Adversary Present	-0.65*	0.23	0.52	-0.39*	0.24	0.68
Relative Present	-0.09	0.28	0.92	0.05	0.29	1.06
Key Citizen/Officer Characteristics						
Indicators of Irrationality				-0.75*	0.12	0.47
Citizen Age				0.18*	0.06	1.19
Officer Minority				-0.20	0.20	0.82
Citizen Minority				-0.09	0.17	0.92
Citizen Low Income				0.03	0.17	1.03
Model X^2	173.09*	17 df		216.33*	22 df	
X^2 Improvement Statistic	54.27*	4 df		43.25*	5 df	
Nagelkerke R^2	.24			.29		

*p < .05, one-tailed

The full model (V) in table 5.6 requires further discussion. Upon examination we observe that all three procedural justice indexes are significantly different than zero. One unit increases of each of the respective measures, holding all else constant, have the following impact: the index of ethicality increases the likelihood of compliance nearly 1.5 times, information seeking increases the likelihood nearly 1.6 times, and the decision-making index increases the likelihood 1.9 times. Only one of the independent variables included in the coercion domain is statistically significant. When the police mention that arrest is a possible choice in the situation (this is measured independent of coercion) then the citizen is nearly 1.6 times more likely to comply with the police request for self-control. With respect to the third party influences, the index and the presence of an adversary are the only significant predictors of citizen compliance. A one unit change in the index generates slightly more than a two-fold increase in citizen compliance, holding all else constant. The presence of an adversary, holding all else constant, makes the target 1.5 times more likely to rebel against the request for self-control. Two citizen characteristics, irrationality and age, are significant predictors of compliance with police requests for self-control in phase I, as indicated in the previous analysis. For every unit increase in the number of irrational elements affecting a citizen, the citizen becomes two times less likely to comply with the police request. For every one unit increase in the age variable, target citizens are 1.19 times more likely to comply with the police request for self-control.

When comparing these models with those estimated without composite indexes we essentially generate a similar story. Consonant with our major theoretical argument, targets are swayed to comply with police requests for self-control by what the police and other citizens do. Police actions that reinforce impartiality and quality decision-making, indicate attentiveness to the situation and the need for informed decision-making, and treat targets in a manner consistent with citizen expectations generate greater levels of compliance.[3] Consistent with social interactionist theory and specifically the hypotheses Milgram (1973) generated, we find that third party behaviors towards police impact targets' decisions to comply. Holding all else constant, a target will be less likely to comply if a confederate is rebelling, but will be more likely to be compliant if a confederate is obedient. The presence of an adversary also dampens the likelihood of citizen compliance. Surprisingly, the coercive power that police bring to bear on a citizen in the form of commanding, handcuffing, arresting and so on, has a minimal impact on citizen's compliance decision. Whether police mention arrest as a possible outcome, regardless of it being accompanied by threats, handcuffing, or suggestion, does impact the decision to comply. This might indicate that when police put the situation in a legal context they may in fact be increasing legitimacy of their presence, however, one cannot minimize the increase in stakes and therefore coercive power that mentioning arrest can have. The uncertainty of the "meaning" of the mentioning of arrests is amplified by the relative lack of any other coercive power indicators to predict compliance. Our post hoc explanation to recast this variable as a measure of legitimacy is made in that context. That irrational citizens are less likely to comply is unsurprising and represents a finding consistent with the idea that those who are affected by alcohol, mental illness, or anger may ignore important cues during social interaction (see e.g. Tedeschi and Felson, 1994). Such impaired perceptions make persuasion via coercion or fair procedure less effective and perhaps less predictable, thus increasing the likelihood of rebellion.

PHASE II OF POLICE-CITIZEN ENCOUNTERS

Our analysis of phase II traces those cases in which police make a second request for self-control in the course of the police-citizen encounter. We document the flow of requests with figure 5.1. Of the 288 citizens who were noncompliant in phase I, 203 (70 percent) of those citizens were asked to exercise self-control in phase II of the encounter. In this group of 203 cases, 142 citizens were compliant by the end of the encounter, which represents a compliance rate of 70 percent among those originally rebelling against police authority. Of the 651 citizens who were compliant in phase I, 90 (14 percent) were asked by police to exercise self-control a second time. Of these 90 cases in our sample, only nine citizens (10 percent) did not comply with the police request. This indicates that once police have established compliant behavior with their requests they are extremely likely to receive it again when they ask citizens for further compliance.

Options for multivariate analysis of 90 cases, where only 9 citizens rebel are extremely limited. Since our goal was at the outset was to explore the pathways through which police obtain compliance or rebellion, we include these 90 cases in an analysis with those who were non-compliant, and include a dummy indicator of whether the target in phase II was compliant with the phase I request. This represents a stability coefficient to control for behavior in phase I. We will then present models of only those citizens who were non-compliant in phase I as a comparison to this baseline.

Figure 5.1

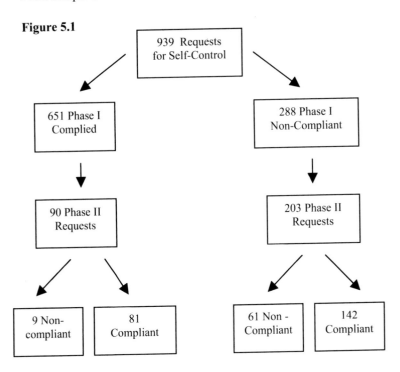

Phase II Descriptives

As an initial step in analyzing phase II data, we first present the descriptive statistics for the phase II dependent variable which measures compliance with requests for self-control. We then turn our attention to independent measures, addressing variables in time order and theoretical centrality to our investigation. We begin with entry tactics and the target's phase I response; next we discuss procedural justice indicators, coercion, third party influences, and finally the key characteristics of citizens and officers. Our descriptive statistics are presented in table 5.7. An exhaustive treatment of possible measures is presented in that table. Measures with limited variance (less than 5 percent) are excluded from the analysis, unless they are included in indexes representing key concepts. The indexes that we adopt for this analysis are identical to those used in the second phase I analysis. The limited sample size requires this compromise to obtain meaningful statistical estimates of phase II compliance. Only those variables that will be included in phase II will be described below.

Table 5.7 Descriptive Statistics for Phase II Variables (n=293)

	Min.	Max.	Mean	S.D.
Citizen Compliant (0=no, 1=yes)	0	1	0.76	0.43
Independent Variables				
Police Entry	0	5	1.39	0.93
Indicators of Procedural Justice				
Citizen Entry (Rectitude) (0=no, 1=yes)	0	1	0.01[a]	0.10
Citizen Entry (Morality) (0=no, 1=yes)	0	1	0.02[a]	0.13
Police Respect Citizen (0=no, 1=yes)	0	1	0.20[x]	0.40
Police Disrespect Citizen (0=no, 1=yes)	0	1	0.12[x]	0.33
Citizen has Voice (0=no, 1=yes)	0	1	0.21[x]	0.41
Citizen's Voice Terminated (0=no, 1=yes)	0	1	0.09[x]	0.29
Index of Ethicality	-2	2	0.19	0.78
Police Seek Information: Identity (0=no, 1=yes)	0	1	0.13[x]	0.33
Police Seek Information: Situation (0=no, 1=yes)	0	1	0.16[x]	0.36
Police Seek Information: Solution (0=no, 1=yes)	0	1	0.06[x]	0.23
Index of Information Seeking	0	2	0.34	0.60
Police Indicate Bias (0=no, 1=yes)	0	1	0.04[x]	0.20
Police Indicate Leniency (0=no, 1=yes)	0	1	0.04[x]	0.21

	Min.	Max.	Mean	S.D.
Police Indicate Independence (0=no, 1=yes)	0	1	0.06^x	0.23
Index of Decision-Making	-1	1	0.06	0.37
Police have Probable Cause (0=no, 1=yes)	0	1	0.09	0.29
Indicators of Police Coercion				
Police Mention Arrest (0=no, 1=yes)	0	1	0.23	0.42
Police Make Suggestion (0=no, 1=yes)	0	1	0.05^x	0.21
Police Command (0=no, 1=yes)	0	1	0.27^x	0.44
Police Threaten (0=no, 1=yes)	0	1	0.21^x	0.41
Citizen Handcuffed (0=no, 1=yes)	0	1	0.06^x	0.25
Citizen Searched (0=no, 1=yes)	0	1	0.05^x	0.21
Physical Force v Citizen (0=no, 1=yes)	0	1	0.08^x	0.27
Gender Dyad	1	3	1.92	0.60
Citizen Arrested (0=no, 1=yes)	0	1	0.07^x	0.25
Citizen Cited (0=no, 1=yes)	0	1	0.02^x	0.15
Citizen has Weapon (0=no, 1=yes)	0	2	0.03^a	0.22
Number of Police Present (square root)	0	1.73	0.30	0.51
Number of Citizens Present (square root)	0	9.95	1.20	1.19
Police Command Self Control (0=no, 1=yes)	0	1	0.75^x	0.43
Index of Coercive Police Action	0	5	2.19	1.40
Third Party Influences on Target Citizens				
3rd Party Positive Verbalization (0=no, 1=yes)	0	1	0.02^x	0.15
3rd Party Negative Verbalization (0=no, 1=yes)	0	1	0.01^x	0.12
3rd Party Rebellion (0=no, 1=yes)	0	1	0.10^x	0.30
3rd Party Compliant (0=no, 1=yes)	0	1	0.05^x	0.21
Index of 3rd Party Influences	-1	1	0.06	0.40
Relative is Adversary (0=no, 1=yes)	0	1	0.01^a	0.08
Adversary Present (0=no, 1=yes)	0	1	0.03^a	0.17
Relative Present (0=no, 1=yes)	0	1	0.04^a	0.19
Key Citizen and Officer Characteristics				
Indicators of Irrationality	0	3	0.88	0.78
Citizen Age	2	8	5.27	1.44
Officer Minority (0=no, 1=yes)	0	1	0.23	0.42
Citizen Minority (0=no, 1=yes)	0	1	0.59	0.49
Citizen Low Income (0=no, 1=yes)	0	1	0.67	0.47
Citizen Complied in Phase I (0=no, 1=yes)	0	1	0.31	0.46

[a]Indicator excluded due to limited variance, [x] Indicator included in an index variable

Dependent Variable

The dependent variable in phase II represents whether the citizen was compliant with additional self-control requests made by the police. Thus we are moving beyond phase I, and examining whether citizens comply with the police once they have demonstrated a prior valence on their obedience to authority. The phase II dependent variable is also not necessarily a discrete response to a single request, as was the phase I dependent variable. This variable represents whether the citizen was noncompliant with any phase II requests made by the police and represents a composite measure similar to that adopted by Mastrofski and colleagues (1996) in their original work in this area. Of the 293 cases in our phase II sample 223 (76 percent) were compliant with all police requests for self-control in phase II of the encounters.

Independent Variables

Police entry into phase II of the encounter, which like the remainder of the variables in these analyses (unless otherwise noted) is unique to phase II, is the first measure we discuss. It ranges from zero to five (0=passive, 1=ask questions, 2=command, 3=threaten, 4=physical force, 5=arrest) and has a mean of 1.39, the modal tactic was a command, which was the first police action in 43 of the phase II cases. A second variable that must be considered an "entry tactic" is the citizen's prior valence on compliance with police phase I requests. This dummy variable measures whether the citizen complied with the first request for self-control and has a mean level of .31.

Procedural Justice Indicators

We included three procedural justice indexes and the presence of probable cause in the phase II model of citizen compliance. The first variable is the index of ethicality computed using the following formula:

Index of Ethicality =

$$X_{respect} - X_{disrespect} + X_{opportunity\ for\ voice} - X_{termination\ of\ voice}.$$

This measure has a range from –2 to 2 and a mean level of .19. The modal category of this variable is zero, with 59 percent of the sample at that level. The second procedural justice indicator is the index of information seeking which was computed with the following formula:

Index of Information Seeking =

$$X_{info\ on\ identity} + X_{info\ on\ situation} + X_{info\ on\ resolution}.$$

That measure has a range of zero to two, with the modal level being zero with 72 percent of the cases. The third indicator of procedural justice is the index of decision-making measured with the following formula:

Index of Decision-making quality = $X_{leniency} - X_{bias} + X_{independence}.$

This variable has a range of –1 to 1 and a modal level of zero, with 86 percent of the cases falling in that category. The final indicator of procedural justice is a variable that represents whether the police generated probable cause against the suspect in phase II. In nine percent of the sample cases police generated probable cause for target law breaking in phase II.

Coercion

We measure five variables representing coercive power in phase II of the police-citizen encounters in our sample. First, we measure whether the police mentioned arrest as a possible outcome of the situation which occurred in 23 percent of the phase II cases. Our rationale is similar to phase I where we argued that mentioning arrest, regardless of whether it is suggested or threatened, may change the target calculus. In addition, the index of police coercion was generated by coding an ordinal variable indicating the most coercive tactic that police made during phase II of the encounter. To construct an index of coercive police actions we chose to adopt the scheme used in phase I: passive (0), suggestions (1), commands (2), threats (3), handcuffing, searching, or physical force (4), arrest or cite (5) as the highest action.

Gender dyad is also included in our model. This variable has a range of 1 to 3, with identical categories as presented in phase I. The modal category of the phase II sample is also same gender dyads, with 63 percent of these cases falling in that category. Two other variables, the square-root transformed measures of additional citizens and police on scene are included as theoretically important carry-overs from phase I (e.g. Muir, 1977). The weakness of these measures is that they reflect only Phase I conditions, due to the relatively vague nature of the narrative data regarding the presence of citizens, outside of the initial count. Nevertheless these two measures are theoretically important and included in our model. The transformed citizen measure has a range of 0 to 9.95 and a mean level of 1.20. The transformed police measure ranges from zero to 1.73 and has a mean level of .30.

Third Party Influences

We include only one measure of third party influence in this model, the index of third party influences computed using the following formula:

Index of 3rd Party = $x_{positive\ verbal} - x_{negative\ verbal} + x_{compliant} - x_{rebels}$.

This variable has a range of –1 to 1 and a mean level of .06. The modal category is zero, with 84 percent of the cases falling at that level.

Key Citizen and Officer Characteristics

Five citizen and officer characteristics were measured to model target compliance with requests for self-control in this sample. Each of these measures was compiled from the observational data coded by the observers. First we measure the number of irrational elements the target is operating under, identical to phase I by summing the number of irrational factors influencing the citizen. This variable ranges from zero to three has a mean of .88 and 34 percent of the target citizens in the sample had no irrational influences affecting their behavior. The modal category for this variable was one irrational element, which was present in 46 percent of the phase II sample cases.

The second measure of individual characteristics is the citizen's age, which is an eight category variable ranging from one to eight with a mean of 5.27, and was coded by trained observers at the time of the encounter. This variable subdivides chronological age into broad categories (1=5 and under (a category in which no phase II cases fell); 2=6-12 years; 3=13-17; 4=18-20; 5=21-29; 6=30-44; 7=45-59; 8=60 and above). The modal age range represents adults 30 to 44, comprising 39 percent of the sample.

Minority status of the observed officer is measured by a dummy variable and indicates that 23 percent of the phase II sample encounters involved minority officers. Similarly, a dummy variable is used to measure whether the target was a member of a minority group. This sample of citizens asked to control their behaviors is composed of 59 percent minority targets. Our dummy variable indicating chronic poverty or lower income citizens as low income (1) and middle and upper class citizens as the reference (0) category indicates that 67 percent of the citizens in the phase II sample were low income.

Modeling Phase II Compliance

Our models of citizen compliance in phase II of the encounters are presented in tables 5.8a and 5.8b. We replicated the model building scheme used in our phase I analyses, which steps in domains in sequential order. Below we will briefly discuss the model diagnostics for each domain, and reserve the treatment of specific parameters for the full model. In model I, (not presented in table, consistent with our previous analyses), we use police entry tactics in phase II and citizen's compliance in phase I as predictors of phase II compliance. The model chi-square (x^2 =15.16, 2 d.f.) indicates that those variables provide a significant improvement over chance. Citizen compliance in phase I is a significant and positive predictor.   In model II (presented in table 5.8a) we enter a block of four procedural justice indicators, and the likelihood ratio test chi-square statistic (x^2 =3.19, 4 d.f.) indicates this block does not improve prediction of phase II compliance beyond chance. Model III enters a block of indicators of coercion and the chi-squared improvement statistic (x^2 =33.89, 5 d.f.) indicates the block provides significant improvement beyond that expected by chance.

Model IV adds one variable, the index of third party influences, and the chi-squared improvement statistic (x^2 =6.17, 1 d.f.) indicates that the inclusion of that variable provides significant improvement to the model of phase II compliance. Finally, we entered a block of police and citizen characteristics which did not generate a significant chi-squared improvement statistic (x^2 =9.08, 5 d.f.).

The full model (V: presented in table 5.8b) provides us with an opportunity to examine the relative impacts of the independent variables on the likelihood of compliance with phase II requests for self-control.   The model fit statistic (x^2 =67.96, 17 d.f.) indicates that the full model is a significant improvement over chance prediction of target compliance.   In examining the individual predictors we find divergence from phase I compliance explanations.   In phase II, coercive police actions are significant predictors of target compliance.   When police mention arrest, holding all else constant, they increase the likelihood of compliance more than three and a half times.   Contrary to our theoretical foundation, the higher the level of coercive action displayed by police, the less likely targets are to comply in phase II. For every one unit increase the index of coercion citizens are about twice as likely to rebel against the self-control request.   A key concern with opposite signs associated with variables that both measure aspects of police coercion in phase II is the presence of collinearity between these two variables.   But as indicated in table 5.9 there is no sign of that problem when one examines the diagnostic statistics associated with the two measures.

Table 5.8a Phase II Compliance Cases (n=293)

	Model II			Model III		
	B	**S.E.**	**Exp(B)**	**B**	**S.E.**	**Exp(B)**
Constant	0.94*	0.30	2.56	2.01*	0.65	7.43
Phase II Entry Tactics	-0.02	0.16	0.98	0.13	0.17	1.14
Citizen Compliance Phase I	1.31*	0.39	3.71	1.43*	0.41	4.17
Indicators of Procedural Justice						
Index of Ethicality	0.18	0.18	1.20	0.09	0.20	1.09
Index of Information Seeking	-0.05	0.24	0.95	0.16	0.26	1.17
Index of Decision-Making	-0.24	0.37	0.78	-0.23	0.42	0.80
Police have Probable Cause	-0.52	0.46	0.59	0.04	0.52	1.04
Indicators of Police Coercion						
Police Mention Arrest				0.99*	0.39	2.70
Index of Coercive Police Action				-0.62*	0.13	0.54
Gender Dyad				-0.10	0.25	0.90
Number of Police Present (sqrt)				-0.32	0.30	0.73
Number of Citizens Present (sqrt)				0.13	0.14	1.14
Third Party Influences on Targets						
Index of 3rd Party Influence						
Citizen and Officer Characteristics						
Indicators of Irrationality						
Citizen Age						
Officer Minority						
Citizen Minority						
Citizen Low Income						
Model X^2	18.81*	6 df		52.70*	11 df	
X^2 Improvement Statistic	3.19	4 df		33.89*	5 df	
Nagelkerke R^2	.09			.25		

*$p < .05$, one tailed test

Table 5.8b Phase II Compliance Cases, Model IV – V (n=293)

	Model IV			Model V		
	B	**S.E.**	**Exp(B)**	**B**	**S.E.**	**Exp(B)**
Constant	1.84*	0.66	6.28	1.81*	0.97	6.09
Entry Tactics	0.08	0.17	1.09	0.13	0.17	1.14
Citizen Compliance Phase I	1.37*	0.41	3.93	1.42*	0.43	4.13
Indicators of Procedural Justice						
Index of Ethicality	0.12	0.20	1.13	0.05	0.20	1.05
Index of Information Seeking	0.18	0.26	1.20	0.17	0.27	1.18
Index of Decision-Making	-0.14	0.43	0.87	-0.12	0.43	0.89
Police have probable cause	0.07	0.52	1.07	0.10	0.54	1.10
Indicators of Police Coercion						
Police Mention Arrest	1.03*	0.39	2.81	1.27*	0.42	3.58
Index of Coercive Police Action	-0.59*	0.13	0.55	-0.57*	0.14	0.57
Gender Dyad	-0.03	0.26	0.97	-0.27	0.28	0.77
Number of Police Present (sqrt)	-0.41	0.31	0.66	-0.43	0.32	0.65
Number of Citizens Present (sqrt)	0.15	0.15	1.16	0.19	0.16	1.21
Third Party Influences on Targets						
Index of 3rd Party Influence	1.01*	0.43	2.75	0.96	0.44	2.60
Citizen and Officer Characteristics						
Indicators of Irrationality				-0.32*	0.23	0.72
Citizen Age				0.11	0.12	1.12
Officer Minority				0.93*	0.44	2.52
Citizen Minority				0.10	0.33	1.11
Citizen Low Income				-0.33	0.37	0.72
Model X^2	58.88*	12 df		67.96*	17df	
X^2 Improvement Statistic	6.17*	1 df		9.08	5 df	
Nagelkerke R^2	.27			.31		

*p < .05, one tailed test

In terms of procedural justice, it appears that no "fair" police effort has an effect that is distinguishable from zero. Third party influence continue to exhibit the impact we found in our phase I analyses. For every unit increase in the third party index the likelihood of compliance increases 2.6 times. With respect to citizen and officer characteristics our results are somewhat at odds with the phase I models. For every irrational element that affects a target citizen the likelihood of compliance is reduced approximately 1.4 times, holding all else constant. In contrast to our phase I findings, minority officers are significantly more likely to obtain compliance in phase II than their white counterparts. Holding all else constant, minority officers are 2.5 times more likely than white officers to obtain citizen compliance in phase II. Finally, citizens who are compliant in phase I, and are subsequently asked for self-control again in the course of the encounter, are four times more likely to comply with phase II requests than those who were not compliant in phase I.

Collinearity diagnostics that are presented in table 5.9 indicate that these variables do not suffer from any detectable collinearity problems. One cautionary note on the interpretation of these models is that we combined both compliant and non-compliant individuals into one model. The nature of the phase I response could, arguably, have an interactive effect with some other variables. To address this issue we assembled a model and removed all phase I compliant citizens from the sample; this generated the model presented in table 5.10. Upon examination, the differences between the two models are minimal. The impact of mentioning arrest, third party influence, and minority officers is in the same direction but slightly more powerful in predicting compliance. The index of coercion and has a slightly less powerful impact in the reduced sample. Only the number of irrational indicators appears to have a significantly different effect across models. In the reduced model it is no longer statistically significant and its sign changed. With respect to our overall interpretation, however, we still find that procedural justice is unimportant, but coercion and third party effects do matter.

An additional concern that these models are unable to address is the cumulative or lagged effects that might be present from phase I actions. As noted we lack a large sample, so the inclusion of phase I constructs in our model of phase II is untenable. It does, however, seem plausible that phase I effects may impact the citizen's ultimate decision to decide in phase II. Different data, with a more substantial number of phase II cases, would be necessary to test such hypotheses.

Table 5.9 Phase II Collinearity Diagnostics (n=293)

	Sqrt:VIF
Phase II Entry Tactics	1.08
Citizen Compliance Phase I	1.06
Indicators of Procedural Justice	
Index of Ethicality	1.06
Index of Information Seeking	1.07
Index of Decision-Making	1.03
Police have Probable Cause	1.05
Indicators of Police Coercion	
Police Mention Arrest	1.06
Index of Coercive Police Action	1.14
Gender Dyad	1.07
Number of Police Present (sqrt)	1.04
Number of Citizens Present (sqrt)	1.08
Third Party Influences on Targets	
Index of 3rd Party Influence	1.04
Key Citizen and Officer Characteristics	
Indicators of Irrationality	1.14
Citizen Age	1.13
Officer Minority	1.08
Citizen Minority	1.05
Citizen Low Income	1.07

Table 5.10 Phase I Noncompliant Citizens in Phase II (n=203)

	B	**S.E.**	**Exp(B)**	**Sqrt:VIF**
Constant	0.63	1.06	1.87	
Phase II Entry Tactics	0.05	0.20	1.05	1.07
Indicators of Procedural Justice				
Index of Ethicality	0.14	0.22	1.15	1.09
Index of Information Seeking	0.34	0.30	1.40	1.06
Index of Decision-Making	0.12	0.47	1.13	1.03
Police have Probable Cause	0.36	0.63	1.44	1.05
Indicators of Police Coercion				
Police Mention Arrest	1.48*	0.46	4.41	1.06
Index of Coercive Police Action	-0.45*	0.14	0.64	1.15
Gender Dyad	-0.23	0.30	0.79	1.08
Number of Police Present (sqrt)	-0.27	0.36	0.77	1.07
Number of Citizens Present (sqrt)	0.23	0.17	1.25	1.10
Third Party Influences on Targets				
Index of 3rd Party Influence	1.58*	0.53	4.85	1.05
Key Citizen and Officer Characteristics				
Indicators of Irrationality	0.07	0.26	1.07	1.13
Citizen Age	0.14	0.13	1.15	1.13
Officer Minority	1.19*	0.50	3.29	1.08
Citizen Minority	0.37	0.37	1.45	1.05
Citizen Low Income	-0.43	0.40	0.65	1.07
Model x^2	46.40*	16 df		
Nagelkerke R^2	.29			

*$p < .05$, one tailed test

DISCUSSION

This chapter examined the likelihood of citizen compliance with self-control requests in the context of police-citizen encounters. Our models indicate that, with respect to the first time a request for self-control is made, the likelihood of citizen compliance is strongly affected by procedurally just tactics and third party behaviors that can be modeled by the targets. Irrational and youthful citizens also appear to be less likely to acquiesce to police requests the first time they are made, but overall police and citizen characteristics do not figure prominently in the models. Given the centrality of coercive power to the culture of policing (e.g., Paoline, 2003), it has surprisingly little impact on whether citizens obey these first requests for self-control.

Once we move to subsequent requests for self-control that are made in these encounters we find that procedural fairness no longer has a significant impact on target compliance. The behavior of third parties, with respect to providing models to emulate, does significantly impact the likelihood of compliance for subsequent requests. The variable that measures highest level of police coercion in phase II has a counterintuitive impact on compliance, in that higher levels of coercion beget lower levels of cooperation. Rebellion in the face of coercion does not comport with the hypotheses generated from the social interactionist perspective (Tedeschi and Felson 1994; cf. Molm 1997). Whether the police mention arrest, regardless of its context in a suggestion, comment, or threat, does increase citizen compliance significantly. The possibility of arrest (not yet executed) may alter the calculus of the target citizen and increase his stake in conformity, which is consonant with the hypotheses generated by Tedeschi and Felson (1994).

Two questions are left unanswered by this chapter. First, we are uncertain whether procedural justice figures as prominently into other choices citizens may make in the face of police requests. Chapter six will explore how citizens, in street stops, respond to the request for information. The analyses we have conducted here have examined the responses police obtain for quasi-judicial "verdicts" rendered in every day encounters. Whether this generalizes to other police-citizen interactions is an open question. Second, we must explore factors that may condition the interpretation of police actions in the context of these encounters. Chapter seven takes aim at four possible conditioning variables that may have interactive relationships with the models we outline in this chapter. These include the neighborhood distress level, the presence of probable cause, and the presence of an adversary, and whether the citizen is operating under the influence of any irrational elements.

CHAPTER SIX
REQUESTS FOR IDENTIFICATION: MEASURES AND MODELS

This chapter attempts to identify the tactical choices of police that influence the likelihood of citizens cooperating in providing identifying information when requested by the police.   Sykes and Brent's (1983) research indicates that police work is reliant upon asking questions repeatedly, however, there is some reason to suppose that cooperation with these police requests may not be governed by procedural concerns on the part of citizens. The street stops that we have chosen for analysis and requests for identification represent situations where police legitimacy is tenuous (National Advisory Commission, 1968: 303) but not necessarily comparable to requests for self-control. Seeking of information is more akin to establishing interaction and rapport, except perhaps in cases of interrogation, and not equivalent with asking a suspect to control himself. The latter request is an example of police making a quasi-judicial decision on scene. Requests for identification are, we argue, less apt to generate a concern for "just decision-making" since they represent fact seeking and not an outcome or disposition. The theory that we outlined thus far fits best with requests for social control; nevertheless, investigating whether justice concerns, coercion, or third parties influence decisions to comply with requests for identification is important, but requires a more conservative approach to theory testing. Hence, we argue for a more conservative two-tailed test in examining our models for significant predictors of compliance. Requests for self-control are directly analogous to judicial verdicts, but requests for identification are more like discovery or cross-examination. Thus, we caution on the side of null findings, since our theoretical foundation may be weaker.

In drawing a sample of cases to analyze we created a file that consisted of proactively encountered suspects involved in non-traffic situations to establish the types of street stops that the National Advisory Commission (1968) found to be so potentially explosive. We narrowed the pool of cases by limiting the sample of encounters to those involving both non-traffic situations and those instances where the contact with the suspect is police initiated. We compiled all suspects and disputants encountered by the police, where the observed officer was in the decision making lead (n=3,128) then eliminated those that were involved in encounters that were coded as traffic stops or involved reactive police contact (e.g. a response to a call). The coded data from the Project on Policing Neighborhoods, collected by trained observers, allowed us to perform a computer selection of these cases. Of all citizens encountered there were 793 cases in which the problem was not a traffic stop and the police made a self initiated contact with the citizen. To further narrow the sample we entered the narrative data into a database program and searched for text strings for the words "license" and "identification," including misspellings and truncations that the field researchers were known to use. This search narrowed the number of cases to 450 instances where police initiated a non-traffic encounter and may have made a request for a license or identification. Upon examining this group of cases we found 343 citizens who were asked for identification or licenses; of that number, 319 had a narrative that was sufficiently detailed to provide a basis for coding and complete information from the coded POPN data. Twenty-two cases were discarded because the narrative was not adequate for determining whether the citizen cooperated or was inadequate for the purposes of coding other variables only a few cases had missing observational data. One concern with this method for identifying cases is that we may have performed an insufficient text search on the cases, but an examination of a small sample of cases in which key search terms were not found revealed no instance of a request for identification from a suspect. Therefore we conclude that the boundary drawn around these kinds of encounters (proactive, non-traffic, identification requested) has been adequately enumerated through this process.

DEPENDENT VARIABLE

The measure of compliance with requests for identification is similar to that discussed for self control requests. Here we also consider cooperative behavior as sufficient for being compliant. For instance, citizens may offer alternate forms of identification to police and that, we argue, should be considered cooperative behavior. For example, a police officer asking a suspect for a license might instead receive verbal information regarding the suspect's social security number, address, or an alternative form of identification. In this analysis we consider that as an example of cooperative citizen behavior since it is analogous to a promise to comply in the future. Only in cases of refusal, totally putting off the request, or ignoring the officer do we consider the request to be one of non-compliance. The dependent variable that we examine first is the citizen's response to a police officer's initial request for identification. In 21 percent of the 319 cases the target citizen ignored or refused to provide information to the police.

INDEPENDENT VARIABLES

Descriptive measures are presented in table 6.1 and will be used for modeling target compliance with requests for identification. Unless noted as a measure taken from the original POPN coded data, each of these measures was hand coded from the narratives written by observers. Variables that have multiple categories are presented in detail to further address the distribution of those variables. Measures that have limited variance, as noted in table 6.1, will be omitted from the discussion of our independent measures since their theoretical importance has been previously discussed but their utility in developing statistical models of compliance, in this sample and regarding this dependent variable, appear severely limited.

    We discuss our independent measures in four broad categories. First, we address entry tactics that police adopted during these street stops. Second, we examine the tactics police may use in street stops that would be considered procedurally fair or unfair in accordance with our prior theoretical arguments. Third, we measure the various forms of coercive actions that police use in encounters with citizens and capture several other important variables that may influence the coercive power of target and requestor. Fourth, we discuss the variables that capture third-party influence on citizens' on scene behavior. Finally, we discuss our measures of key citizen characteristics that may influence the likelihood of compliance.

Table 6.1 Descriptive Statistics for Phase I Analysis (N=319)

	Min.	Max.	Mean	S.D.
Dependent Variable				
Compliance, Request for ID (0=no, 1=yes)	0	1	0.79	0.41
Independent Variables				
Police Entry	1	5	2.37	0.85
Indicators of Procedural Justice				
Police Disrespect Citizen (0=no, 1=yes)	0	1	0.07	0.25
Respectful Towards Citizen (0=no, 1=yes)	0	1	0.07	0.25
Citizen has Voice (0=no, 1=yes)	0	1	0.35	0.48
Citizen's Voice Terminated (0=no, 1=yes)	0	1	0.04^a	0.19
Police Seek Information (0=no, 1=yes)	0	1	0.46	0.50
Police Indicate Bias (0=no, 1=yes)	0	1	0.00^a	0.06
Police Indicate Independence (0=no, 1=yes)	0	1	0.16	0.37
Citizen Entry (Morality) (0=no, 1=yes)	0	1	0.00^a	0.06
Citizen Entry (Rectitude) (0=no, 1=yes)	0	1	0.00^a	0.00
Police have Probable Cause (0=no, 1=yes)	0	1	0.38	0.49
Indicators of Police Coercion				
Police Mention Arrest (0=no, 1=yes)	0	1	0.02^a	0.15
Police Make Suggestion (0=no, 1=yes)	0	1	0.01^a	0.08
Police Command (0=no, 1=yes)	0	1	0.14	0.35
Police Threaten (0=no, 1=yes)	0	1	0.04^a	0.21
Citizen Handcuffed (0=no, 1=yes)	0	1	0.09	0.29
Citizen Searched (0=no, 1=yes)	0	1	0.22	0.41
Physical Force v Citizen (0=no, 1=yes)	0	1	0.05	0.22
Gender Dyad	1	3	1.96	0.53
Citizen Arrested (0=no, 1=yes)	0	1	0.05	0.23
Citizen Cited (0=no, 1=yes)	0	1	0.00^a	0.06
Citizen has Weapon (0=no, 1=yes)	0	1	0.02^a	0.12
Police Present (sqrt)	0	5	0.31	0.82
Citizens Present (sqrt)	0	7	1.11	0.99
Police Command Identification (0=no, 1=yes)	0	1	0.02^a	0.14

	Min.	Max.	Mean	S.D.
Third Party Influences on Target Citizens				
3rd Party Negative Verbalization (0=no, 1=yes)	0	1	0.03[a]	0.18
3rd Party Positive Verbalization (0=no, 1=yes)	0	1	0.01[a]	0.10
3rd Party Rebellion (0=no, 1=yes)	0	1	0.28	0.45
3rd Party Compliant (0=no, 1=yes)	0	1	0.05	0.22
Adversary Present (0=no, 1=yes)	0	1	0.03[a]	0.18
Relative Present (0=no, 1=yes)	0	1	0.04[a]	0.20
Relative is Adversary (0=no, 1=yes)	0	1	0.01[a]	0.08
Key Citizen and Officer Characteristics				
Indicators of Irrationality	0	2	0.32	0.54
Citizen Age	2	8	4.89	1.33
Officer Minority (0=no, 1=yes)	0	1	0.18	0.39
Citizen Minority (0=no, 1=yes)	0	1	0.69	0.46
Citizen Low Income (0=no, 1=yes)	0	1	0.70	0.46

[a] Indicator variables with less than five percent of cases in the "yes" category will be omitted from multivariate analyses due to limited variance

Entry

Police entry tactics are measured by a five-category variable (1=passive 2=ask questions, 3=issue commands, 4=issue threat, 5=physical force, 6=arrested citizen) that ranges from passive action to using physical force on the target citizen (the sixth category, citizen arrested upon entry was not present in this sample). The mean of the variable is 2.37, and the modal category is asking questions. In 221 cases, or about 70 percent of the encounters, the police asked a question on entry. Police issued commands upon entry in 63 encounters or 20 percent of the encounters. Physical force upon entry was the next most common tactic, occurring in nearly seven percent of the sample. Passive behavior by the police was observed in 12 cases or nearly four percent of the encounters. The most rare entry tactic was issuing a threat to the citizens which occurred in only 2 encounters, or less than one percent of the time. This distribution of entry tactics is not surprising given the micro-analysis of police-citizen interaction performed by Sykes and Brent (1980). Asking questions and establishing verbal control of the police-citizen interaction are a primary action of police according to their analysis as well as the ethnographic work of Muir (1977).

Indicators of Procedural Justice

Ten indicators of procedural justice were initially coded, however only six evidenced sufficient variation in this sample to be included in the analyses. Two indicators of police ethicality, whether police were respectful of the target citizen or disrespectful of the target citizen, were each present in seven percent of sample cases. We measured voice as being present when police gave targets an opportunity to talk about the situation prior to asking for identification, which occurred in 35 percent of the sample cases. We measured information seeking by the police as whether police asked questions about the presenting situation, besides those for identification. In 46 percent of the cases police did ask target citizens for information prior to requesting identification. We measured independence of decision making as those instances where police clearly indicated that they were acting under legal guidelines towards the target citizen and in sixteen percent of the sample police indicated to citizens that their actions were based on legal guidelines. Whether police had probable cause to stop the citizen, which would influence the legitimacy of their street stop, was measured as being present when the evidence level rises to two or more points from the following list (scores in parentheses): officer observes violation (2), officer obtains physical evidence implicating citizen (2), officer hears full confession (2), officer hears eyewitness testimony implicating citizen (1), officer hears partial confession (1). This evidence scale is expected to be positively related to the likelihood of compliance. The police had probable cause prior to the request for identification in thirty-eight percent of the street stops in our sample.

Four measures of procedural justice are eliminated from our models of target decision-making due to insufficient variance. Our coding scheme relies heavily on the dummy coding of police tactics or citizen behaviors, and in cases where the tactic or behavior appears in less than five percent of the sample (15 cases out of 319 is approximately five percent), we omit the variable from multivariate analyses. This is a departure from analyses performed on the self-control request sample, but is defensible since this sample is one-third as large. We remove variables with limited variance to ensure model estimation will be possible. Termination of the citizen's voice, as measured by police telling a citizen to be quiet or shut up, was present in only four percent of the sample. Indications that police were biased, exemplified by the verbalization that they are clearly taking "a side" of another party against the target citizen, occurred in less than one percent of the sample cases. Finally, citizen's morality or their belief in the rectitude and legitimacy of police intervention in the presenting situation is measured by positive or negative target utterances prior to any police action. Target citizens' negative utterances, indicating a lack of police "morality," were present in less than one percent of the cases (in fact in only one case did a citizen make a negative statement about the police prior to any police action), and therefore had insufficient variance to be included in our model of target compliance. Statements reflecting positive regard for police, made by targets prior to police action, were not present in any of the 319 sample encounters.

Coercion

Five police tactics are measured using dummy variables (1=tactic used 0=tactic not used) and include commands, handcuffing, searching, physical force, and arresting the target citizen. Prior to requesting identification police commanded the target citizens in fourteen percent of the encounters, handcuffed citizens in nine percent, searched citizens in 22 percent, used physical force in five percent and arrested the target citizen in five percent of the encounters. Gender dyad is a variable measuring the gender relationship between the target and the requestor (1=female target/male requestor, 2=target/requestor same gender, 3=male target/female requestor). This was computed from the coded data collected by the observers regarding the gender of the citizen and surveys conducted by POPN researchers that coded the gender of the observed officer. The mean level of variable is 1.96, and the modal category is target and requestor share the same gender. In sixteen percent of the cases female targets are paired with male police officers and in twelve percent of the cases male citizens are paired with female police officers. We measure the number of officers (besides the observed officer) on scene at the beginning of the encounter with a continuous variable that ranges from zero to five. In 83 percent of the cases there were no other officers on scene and the mean number of officers on scene was .31. Finally, we use a square root transformation of the number of citizens (besides the target) who are on scene at the beginning of the encounter. The untransformed variable ranges from zero to 49, with nearly 75 percent of the cases falling in the first three categories. To address the distribution the variable was transformed, which resulted in a mean level of 1.11 and a range from zero to seven. Both variables, the number of police and the number of citizens on scene at the beginning of the encounter, were taken from the data coded by the observers rather than coded from narratives.

Six variables will not be included in the analysis because of insufficient variation. In this sample the tactics of police mentioning arrest to the target, making suggestions, threatening, issuing a citation, or commanding that identification be given failed to meet our threshold of variation. One other variable, whether the citizen had a weapon, appeared in only two percent of this sample, and therefore is excluded from the analysis.

Third Party Influences

Milgram's work in social psychology indicates the importance of allies, colleagues, or models in guiding one's behavior, especially with regard to obedience to authority figures. Two hypotheses can be drawn from that work, which are germane to the police-citizen encounter. First, if citizens are in the presence of a non-cooperative citizen, then they would be more likely to be disobedient. Conversely one would expect that if target citizens are in the presence of a cooperative third party then they will be more likely to comply. Another consideration of third party influence is whether the target citizen is dealing with someone that could be considered an adversary at the scene and whether the target has a pre-existing relationship with an adversary or non-adversary at the scene. We can measure only two third party variables for our model to determine whether the citizens are more likely to rebel or acquiesce in the presence of other citizens who are rebellious or compliant.

First we measure whether there is a third party present who is rebelling against (ignoring or refusing) a compliance request from the police. In this sample 28 percent of the cases involved a situation where the target was in the presence of another citizen who was openly defying police authority. Second we measure whether a third party is present who is complying with police requests. In this sample five percent of the target citizens were in the presence of a compliant third party.

Five indicators of third party influence on target compliance decisions were excluded from analysis since, despite theoretical importance, they lacked sufficient variation. Third parties that made negative comments about the police were present in only three percent of the cases and third parties making positive statements were present in only one percent of the cases. Three measures that captured the presence of relatives and adversaries at the scene were excluded. The presence of an adversary at the scene of the encounter occurred in only three percent of the sample, the presence of a relative on scene occurred in only four percent of the encounters, and finally the combination of relative-that-is-an-adversary was quite rare, being present in only one percent of the encounters. Such distributions are not surprising given that these encounters are proactive stops of citizens and thus are not likely to involve disputes.

<u>Key Citizen and Officer Characteristics</u>

Five citizen and officer characteristics were measured to model target compliance with requests for identification in this sample. Each of these measures was compiled from the observational data coded by the observers. First we measure the number of irrational elements the target is operating under, including whether the citizen appeared drunk, mentally ill, or under the influence of heightened emotions. An ordinal variable was constructed by summing the number of irrational factors influencing the citizen and ranges from zero to two (in no case in this sample did a citizen have three indicators of irrationality). That measure had a mean of .32 and 71 percent of the target citizens in the sample had no irrational influences affecting their behavior. Of those with one or more factors influencing their behavior five (1.6 percent) had evidence of mental illness, 40 (12.5 percent) had behavioral effects of alcohol or drugs, and 58 (18.2 percent) had evidence of strong emotions or anger as an irrational element in this index.

The second measure of individual characteristics is the citizen's age, which is a seven category variable ranging from two to eight with a mean of 4.89, and was coded by trained observers at the time of the encounter. This variable subdivides chronological age into broad categories (2=6-12 years; 3=13-17; 4=18-20; 5=21-29; 6=30-44; 7=45-59; 8=60 and above). The modal age range represents adults 30 to 44, comprising 31 percent of the sample. Categories three through five, which range from 13 to 29 years old, represent 21 percent, 16 percent, and 23 percent of the target citizens in the sample. Very young targets under 13, and older targets over 45 are limited to less than ten percent of the sample.

Minority status of the observed officer is measured by a dummy variable and indicates that eighteen percent of the target sample encounters involved minority officers. Similarly, a dummy variable is used to measure whether the target was of minority status. This sample of proactive street stops is composed of 69 percent minority target citizens. A measure of income coded by observers who assessed the citizens' level of wealth indicated whether citizens appeared to be in chronic poverty, lower class, or middle class, or upper class (no sample cases involved encounters with citizens with apparent upper class income levels). We collapsed these categories into a dummy variable with chronic poverty and lower income citizens as low income (1) and middle class citizens as the reference (0) category. Of the sample cases 70 percent were coded as low income.

MODELING IDENTIFICATION REQUESTS

Since our dependent variable is binary we use logistic regression models to estimate models of target compliance (Long 1997; Menard 1995). To assess the individual contributions of the domains of variables we have outlined above, we opt to step the variables into a logistic model to determine where significant explanatory power exists. Tables 6.2a and 6.2b contain the results of logistic regression models estimated using cooperation with police requests for identification as the dependent variable during phase I. In the interest of saving space, model I, featuring entry tactics, is presented only in the text. The variables were stepped into the equation using a mixture of event timing and theoretical importance. We entered the following blocks of variables, in this order, into our model: Entry tactics, procedural justice indicators, indicators of coercion, third party influences, and citizen and officer characteristics. To test the significance of each block we use a likelihood ratio chi-square test, which measures whether the block introduces significant improvement over the model omitting that block (Long, 1997: 94-96). The model chi-square is also reported to measure whether the model is a better than chance fit to the data.

The variable measuring entry tactics was entered in model I (not shown) since it captures the first actions of the police on scene. The model chi-square test (x^2=2.86, 1 d.f.) indicates that the model is not a significant improvement over chance. Six indicators of procedural justice are entered on the next step in model II. The chi-square test indicates that the model fit is no better than chance (x^2=5.82, 7 d.f.), and the likelihood ratio test statistic indicates that the block of procedural justice indicators is also non-significant (x^2=2.96, 6 d.f.). With respect to the seven variables in model II we cannot be confident that any of the predictors' betas are different from zero, thus none are interpretable.

Table 6.2a Phase I Logistic Regression Analyses, Model II - III

	Model II			Model III		
	B	**S.E.**	**Exp(B)**	**B**	**S.E.**	**Exp(B)**
Constant	1.85*	0.42		2.07*	0.73	
Police Entry	-0.31*	0.16	0.73	-0.32	0.21	0.73
Procedural Justice Indicators						
Police Disrespect	0.38	0.63	1.46	0.31	0.69	1.36
Police Respect	0.63	0.65	1.89	0.61	0.71	1.85
Citizen has Voice	0.18	0.35	1.19	-0.03	0.38	0.97
Police Seek Information	-0.05	0.34	0.95	0.19	0.36	1.21
Police Indicate Independence	0.01	0.43	1.01	-0.20	0.45	0.82
Police have Probable Cause	0.28	0.30	1.33	0.53	0.35	1.70
Indicators of Coercion						
Police Command				1.37*	0.59	3.94
Police Handcuff				-0.49	0.73	0.61
Police Search				-0.40	0.40	0.67
Police Use Physical force				-0.41	0.69	0.66
Gender Dyad Level				-0.06	0.28	0.94
Police Arrest				-0.40	0.75	0.67
Number Police Present (sqrt)				-0.29	0.17	0.75
Number Citizens Present (sqrt)				-0.03	0.16	0.97
Model X^2	5.82	7 df		21.3	15 df	
LLH Ratio X^2	2.96	6 df		15.5*	8 df	
Nagelkerke R^2	.03			.10		

* $p < .05$ two tailed test

Model III includes eight indicators of coercion in the model, and the model chi-square is not significant (x^2=21.3, 15 d.f.). The likelihood ratio test chi-square statistic is, however, significant (x^2=15.5, 8 d.f.), indicating that, as a block, the indicators of coercion do offer a significant improvement over chance in predicting whether citizens comply with requests for identification. Closer examination of the model reveals that police commands are the sole significant predictor in the model with beta of 1.37 and an odds ratio of 3.94. More simply, holding constant the other 14 factors in this model, in those instances where police use commands against citizens, those citizens are nearly four times more likely to comply with requests for identification. The interpretation of the coefficient for police commands is, however, tentative at best in a model which in an overall sense is non-significant.

Model IV (table 6.2b) includes two indicators of third party influence as a block in the larger model. Neither the model chi-square (x^2=21.96, 17 d.f.) nor the likelihood ratio statistic indicating the improvement achieved by including the block (x^2=0.63, 2 d.f.) are significant. The coefficient for police commands did, however, maintain its significance and the coefficient and odds ratio associated were nearly unchanged from the previous model.

Five indicators of officer and citizen characteristics were added in model V. The model chi-square (x^2=41.63, 22 d.f.) and the likelihood ratio test chi-square (x^2=19.68, 5 d.f.) were both significant for this model. This indicates that the model is a better than chance predictor of citizen compliance and that the citizen characteristics are better than chance predictors of compliance. Only three predictors (police commands, minority citizens, and low income citizens) from this full model can be distinguished as being significantly different from zero. Police use of commands has a beta of 1.49 and an odds ratio of 4.43, which indicates that, holding all else constant in the model, police are nearly four and one-half times more likely to gain citizen compliance when they issue commands prior to a request for identification. Minority citizen status has a beta of –1.39 and an odds ratio of 0.25 which indicates that, holding all else constant, minority citizens are four times more likely to be non-compliant with police requests for identification when compared with white citizens. Low income status has a beta of –0.79 and an odds ratio of 0.46 which indicates that, holding all else constant, low income citizens are twice as likely to be non-compliant with police requests for identification when compared with middle income citizens.

Table 6.2b Phase I Logistic Regression Analyses, Model IV - V

	Model IV			Model V		
	B	**S.E.**	**Exp(B)**	**B**	**S.E.**	**Exp(B)**
Constant	2.04*	0.73		2.83*	1.11	
Police Entry	-0.31	0.22	0.73	-0.34	0.24	0.71
Procedural Justice Indicators						
Police Disrespect	0.35	0.70	1.41	0.74	0.79	2.09
Police Respect	0.59	0.71	1.80	0.65	0.78	1.92
Citizen has Voice	-0.05	0.38	0.96	-0.15	0.40	0.87
Police Seek Information	0.21	0.37	1.24	0.38	0.38	1.47
Police Indicate Independence	-0.28	0.46	0.76	-0.34	0.50	0.72
Police have Probable Cause	0.54	0.35	1.71	0.57	0.37	1.77
Indicators of Coercion						
Police Command	1.37*	0.60	3.95	1.49*	0.64	4.43
Police Handcuff	-0.42	0.75	0.66	-0.15	0.77	0.86
Police Search	-0.43	0.40	0.65	-0.34	0.42	0.71
Police Use Physical force	-0.33	0.70	0.72	-0.33	0.74	0.72
Gender Dyad Level	-0.06	0.28	0.95	0.13	0.30	1.13
Police Arrest	-0.47	0.76	0.63	-0.69	0.77	0.50
Number Police Present (sqrt)	-0.27	0.17	0.76	-0.19	0.18	0.83
Number Citizens Present (sqrt)	-0.05	0.17	0.95	0.07	0.19	1.07
Third Party Influences						
3rd Party Rebellion	0.21	0.38	1.24	0.32	0.40	1.37
3rd Party Compliant	-0.36	0.64	0.70	-0.34	0.69	0.71
Citizen/Officer Characteristics						
Indicators of Irrationality				-0.52	0.29	0.59
Citizen Age				0.10	0.13	1.10
Officer Minority				-0.15	0.40	0.86
Citizen Minority				-1.39*	0.42	0.25
Citizen Low Income				-0.79*	0.38	0.46
Model X²	21.96	17 df		41.63*	22 df	
LLH Ratio X²	0.63	2 df		19.68*	5 df	
Nagelkerke R²	.10			.19		

* p < .05 two tailed test

Categorical independent variables that had limited variance were eliminated from the model, largely because of the risk of complete separation and quasi-complete separation (Menard, 1995). Despite that tactic, collinearity, or the intercorrelation of independent variables is still a threat to the models built in tables 6.2a and 6.2b. The square root of the variance inflation factor is suggested by Fox (1991) as a useful screen for collinearity. Using the criteria established in chapter five (results not shown) we find no evidence of collinearity, though we note that whether police handcuffed the citizen approached cautionary thresholds.

Of the sample of 319 citizens proactively encountered in non-traffic situations and asked for identification, nearly 80 percent complied with the requests for identification. Indicators of entry tactics, procedural justice, coercion, and third party influence were nearly all non-significant; instead the results indicate that citizens' social status plays a large role in the decision to cooperate, at least with respect to a request for identity. How one is treated by police in terms of entry tactics, just procedures, and coercive power, and the influence of other citizens as models, are all poor explanations of citizen cooperation with police requests for identification in our sample. In terms of theory we hypothesized that the opposite should be true, in that self-presentation of police should most strongly condition how citizens behave and citizen characteristics should be weak or non-significant predictors, with perhaps the exception of the number of irrational elements influencing the citizen. At the outset of this chapter concern was expressed that the request for identification, though important, might not be subject to the same predictors as a request for self control. Below we attempt to interpret these results in light of our theoretical framework.

Examining the nature of our dependent variable is necessary to explain this stark divergence from our theoretical foundation. First, requests for identification represent a "processing" phase (see Bayley, 1986) of the police-citizen encounter where information is sought. It is possible that it could be an entry tactic, but it is unlikely to be an exit strategy for a police officer (it seems quite implausible to imagine police doing nothing more once an identification card is produced). Norms of interaction guide these exchanges between police and citizens and perhaps distal characteristics such as race and class carry attitudes about how forthcoming one is to be during encounters with authorities. Other behaviors, such as respect towards authorities might be conditioned by attitudes held by those in less powerful positions in society (e.g., Sykes and Clark 1975; Hagan and Albonetti 1982).[1] Recent analysis of disrespectful behavior towards police by Reisig, McCluskey, Mastrofski, and Terrill (2003) indicates that class and race, holding constant police actions, are significant predictors of citizen disrespect of police during face to face encounters. How one responds in terms of deference and cooperation with authorities might be linked to how one interacts with authority. A correlation between class and race and an intervening attitude toward authority which motivates defiance would explain why disrespect (Reisig and colleagues, 2003) and cooperation with requests for identification in the present analysis are linked back to the social status of the target.

Second, our theory is rooted strongly in procedural justice concerns of citizens, which are more closely tied to compliance with the law (e.g. Tyler, 1990) than cooperation with processing. Since our primary dependent variable of interest is compliance with a police request for self-control we are more confident that there is a tight fit between those indicators and that outcome. The police, in requesting self-control, are adopting a form of exit strategy that can be likened to a verdict for the police-citizen encounter. They act as a judge in comparing citizen behavior to a legal standard, weigh on scene evidence, and render a decision that the target shall leave the scene, leave another person alone, cease disorderly behavior, or cease illegal behavior. Cooperation with these police decisions, we argue, is more likely to hinge on how a citizen is treated than cooperation with a request for identification, which is neither an exit strategy nor a quasi-verdict bringing an end to an encounter.

Phase II Identification Requests

Encounters between police and citizens were divided into two phases, those events leading up to a compliance request and a citizen's response, and those events that occur subsequent to the initial (in those cases where there are more than one request) police request and citizen response to a compliance demand. Having examined phase I of the proactive street stops we turn our attention to phase II. In the case of proactive street stops we must first address our sample, which is necessarily truncated since those who cooperated with the police will likely be excluded from the sample. Similar to a decision tree, we proposed to examine citizens in compliance and their responses to a second request and citizens in rebellion and their response to a second compliance request. The initial sample size of 319 already has proven to be prohibitive in terms of the variation in independent variables that was lacking in many measures and those concerns mount in this second phase. The outcome of the encounters, in terms of citizen compliance with police requests for identification, is presented in figure 6.1.

Figure 6.1: Distributions of Citizen Compliance Pathways Across Phases

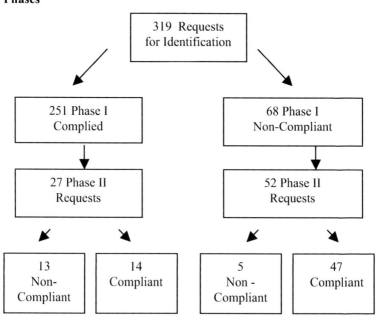

The flow of compliance with identification requests indicates that nearly every citizen asked for identification was ultimately cooperative, in the sense of providing information about themselves, identification cards, or licenses to the police. Our analysis of initial requests indicated that citizens were not forthcoming in about 21 percent of these stops. By the end of the encounter however, 284 of the citizens, or 89 percent were ultimately compliant with the request for identification. Interestingly, when citizens who were compliant with an initial request for identification were pressed for further information on their identity (e.g. confirmation of information such as date of birth) only half complied. Conversely, in 52 of the 68 cases where a citizen was non-compliant in phase I, the police repeated the request and in 91 percent of the cases citizens eventually cooperated.

Due to the limited number of cases that we have in which 27 compliant citizens were asked for further identification or information about their identities and 52 non-compliant citizens were asked for identification, we limit our second phase analysis to a bivariate analysis. In particular, we examine only those variables that were significant in phase I through a series of contingency tables. We will explore whether police use of commands in phase II, citizen minority status, and citizen income continue to influence decision-making in phase II of the encounters. Unfortunately, we are unable to hold constant other factors; therefore the analysis of phase II requests is not as exhaustive as the phase I analyses.

Table 6.3 and 6.4 present the three significant phase I predictors in contingency tables predicting the likelihood of compliance in phase II. None of the three is useful in explaining why citizens who were compliant in phase I remain compliant in phase II when police continue to press them for information. In those instances where citizens ignored or refused cooperation in phase I, however, minority citizens are significantly more likely to acquiesce if the police continue to request information about a suspect's identity. Citizen cooperation, in terms of information giving at least, appears to be readily forthcoming in proactive street stops observed in St. Petersburg and Indianapolis. Taking these encounters on a whole, initial compliance is predicted by commands from police, and citizen income and minority status. Of those who are non-compliant and receive further requests of the police a great majority (90 percent) comply.

Table 6.3   Phase I Compliant Citizens

		Phase II Compliance		
		No	Yes	Total
Phase II Police Command	No	13	14	27
	Yes	0	0	0
Citizen Minority	No	7	6	13
	Yes	6	8	14
Citizen Low Income	No	5	3	8
	Yes	8	11	19
	Total	13	14	27

Table 6.4   Phase I Non-Compliant Citizens

		Phase II Compliance		
		No	Yes	Total
Phase II Police Command	No	5	44	49
	Yes	0	3	3
Citizen Minority[a]	No	2	3	5
	Yes	3	44	47
Citizen Low Income	No	0	8	8
	Yes	5	39	44
	Total	5	47	52

[a]Significant difference between categories

Alternative Analytic Strategies

Alternative analytical choices can be justified for modeling citizen decision-making in phase I and phase II. Above we have chosen to include variables with sufficient variance in phase I and to opt for an exploration of bivariate relationships that were important in phase I through to phase II of the police-suspect encounters. Two other choices are open to the analyst in these situations. First, to avoid excluding the large number of relatively invariant independent variables in phase I, one could opt to create indices of procedural justice indicators, coercion indicators, and third party influence indicators. Second, one could opt to model, as one group, those cases that move forward from phase I identification requests to phase II identification requests. Below we briefly treat these two alternatives and discuss the results obtained when performing such analyses.

Phase I Re-analysis

Coding of independent variables for the 319 cases yielded fifteen variables that we considered as having insufficient variance to be included in the model. Especially in the case of logistic modeling, dichotomous variables can generate quasi-complete separation and impact the overall model (Menard, 1995). Thus we chose to avoid such problems by excluding arguably important predictors on the basis of lack of variance in those independent measures. One could, alternatively, construct an index of domains by summing the indicator variables within each or in the case of coercion, selecting the highest level of police coercion prior to the request for identification. For example, a procedural justice index could be generated by summing up indicators that are, arguably, associated with enhancing the legitimacy of police presence and subtracting those which detract from the legitimacy of police presence. The shortcoming of this approach is that one gets a theoretically nebulous variable that represents a multitude of procedural justice dimensions. This represents a sacrifice when compared to the alternative of entering very precise indicators of police action (albeit with little variance) into a model of compliance.

Table 6.5 Phase I Indices Descriptive Statistics (n=319)

	Min.	Max.	Mean	S.D.
Index of Ethicality	-1	2	0.32	0.62
Index of Legitimacy	-1	3	1.00	0.90
Index of 3rd Party Indicators	-3	2	-0.29	0.59
Index of Police Coercion	0	6	1.36	2.04

Phase I index creation revolved around the decision to maximize the use of indicators of procedural justice, third party influences, and coercion to see whether an alternate model might reduce the impact of citizen characteristics. As noted previously, the request for identification occurs early in police-citizen interaction and separate measures of police actions may have limited variance, whereas a composite measure may offer an opportunity to generate a summary of police actions that will have greater variance and possibly increased explanatory power. With respect to procedural justice we chose to have one index representing ethicality and voice concerns and a second generally indicating the residual procedural justice indicators. The residual index is a departure from construction used in chapter five but is necessary since two fewer items (request for identification and leniency) are in the procedural justice domain. To generate an index of ethicality we took the dummy variables representing police respect, police disrespect, whether the police gave the target an opportunity for voice, and police termination of voice using the following formula:

Index of Ethicality =

$$X_{\text{respect}} - X_{\text{disrespect}} + X_{\text{opportunity for voice}} - X_{\text{termination of voice}}.$$

A second index of procedurally just actions, which we term the index of residual legitimacy, was created by summing the variables for police seeking information, police indicating bias, police indicating independence, and the presence of probable cause using the following formula:

Index of Residual Legitimacy =

$$X_{\text{seek information}} - X_{\text{bias}} + X_{\text{independence}} + X_{\text{probable cause}}.$$

Two variables which had no variance, rectitude and morality, are excluded from the indexes. We argue for two indices since voice concerns and ethicality, in our interpretation of procedural justice literature such as Lind and Tyler (1988), are very closely related in terms of their relationship to behavioral norms that humans expect when interacting with an authority. The second index captures what we would argue are a larger complex of legitimate actions. Whether police are impartial, seek information on which to base decisions, base decisions in law, and have probable cause to intervene all represent facets of the police-citizen encounter that could generate, or undermine a sense of legitimate behavior as perceived by the target citizen.

To construct an index of coercive police actions we chose to code the highest level of coercion present prior to the request for identification, net of the entry tactics. This ordinal variable captures whether the police used no action (0), suggestions (1), commands (2), threats (3), handcuffing or searching (4), arrest or cite (5), or physical force (6) as the highest action.

To capture third party influences on target's compliance we constructed an index using third party negative and positive verbalization, third party compliance and third party rebellion, as well as whether an adversary was present. This index was constructed using the following formula:

Index of 3rd Party =

$$X_{positive\ verbal} - X_{negative\ verbal} + X_{compliant} - X_{rebels} - X_{adversary}.$$

The index of ethicality has a range from negative one to two, a mean of .32 and 60 percent of cases have the modal value of zero. The index of legitimacy ranges from negative one to three, has a mean of one and 42 percent of the cases fall in the modal value of one. The index of third party indicators ranges from negative two to three, has a mean of -.29, and 67 percent of the cases fall in the modal category of zero. Finally the index of police coercion ranges from zero to six, has a mean of 1.36, and 67 percent of the cases fall in the modal category of zero.

Logistic models were estimated replacing individual variables with their composite indices. Those models also included variables, such as gender dyad, number of officers, and so on, which were not included in the indices when entering the respective domains. We chose to replicate the initial logistic models by stepping in domains of variables in an identical sequence of entry tactics, procedural justice indicators, indicators of coercion, the actions of third parties, and key characteristics of targets and police. Results of the logistic regressions are reported in table 6.6a and 6.6b. Model I (not shown) is identical model I from the previous analyses.

Models II through IV do no better than chance at predicting whether citizens complied with requests for identification. In these models only the number of police at the scene is a significant predictor of citizen compliance. The relative weakness of models III and IV indicate that the significance of that coefficient might be due to chance. The indices of ethicality, legitimacy, coercion, and third party influences are not significant in any model. Only model V, the full model, is interpretable since the model chi-square (x^2=30.94, 13 d.f.) is significant and the likelihood ratio test (x^2=18.43, 5 d.f.) indicates that the domain of key citizen and officer characteristics produces a significantly better fit. In this final model, only citizen minority status and income are significant predictors of compliance with requests for identification, holding all else constant.

Table 6.6a Alternative Modeling, Phase I Compliance, Model II-III

	Model II			Model III		
	B	**S.E.**	**Exp(B)**	**B**	**S.E.**	**Exp(B)**
Constant	1.78*	0.41		1.84*	0.68	
Police Entry Level	-0.26	0.15	0.77	-0.10	0.18	0.90
Procedural Justice Indicators						
Index of Ethicality	0.13	0.23	1.14	0.10	0.23	1.10
Index of Legitimacy	0.12	0.16	1.13	0.16	0.17	1.17
Indicators of Coercion						
Index of Police Coercion				-0.09	0.08	0.92
Gender Dyad				-0.11	0.27	0.89
Police Present (sqrt)				-0.39*	0.15	0.68
Citizens Present (sqrt)				0.03	0.15	1.03
Model X^2	3.94	3 df		12.30	7 df	
LLH Ratio X^2	1.08	2 df		8.36	4 df	
Nagelkerke R^2	.02			.06		

* p < .05 two tailed test

The use of the indexes of ethicality, legitimacy, third party influence, and coercive power of the requestor do little to change the outcome of the models. Citizen characteristics of minority status and income level maintain their power in predicting why citizens obey the first request for identification made by the police, and the coefficients, standard errors, and odds ratios associated with those two variables are nearly identical to those produced in our initial models. This leads us to conclude that the estimates in the original model, even excluding some important predictors with limited variance, are relatively stable. The reestimated models with indexes do not change the interesting finding that citizen characteristics appear to play an important role in shaping whether one complies with a police request for identification the first time it is asked of a target. Minority citizens and lower income citizens are significantly less cooperative in these instances than their white and higher income counterparts.

Table 6.6b Alternative Modeling of Phase I Compliance, Model IV - V

	Model IV			Model V		
	B	**S.E.**	**Exp(B)**	**B**	**S.E.**	**Exp(B)**
Constant	1.82*	0.68		1.90*	1.02	
Police Entry Level	-0.10	0.18	0.90	-0.03	0.19	0.97
Procedural Justice Indicators						
Index of Ethicality	0.09	0.24	1.10	-0.02	0.24	0.98
Index of Legitimacy	0.15	0.17	1.17	0.24	0.18	1.27
Indicators of Coercion						
Index of Police Coercion	-0.09	0.08	0.92	-0.08	0.08	0.92
Gender Dyad	-0.11	0.28	0.90	0.05	0.29	1.05
Police Present (sqrt)	-0.38*	0.16	0.69	-0.30	0.16	0.74
Citizens Present (sqrt)	0.01	0.16	1.01	0.16	0.18	1.18
Third Party Influences						
Index of 3rd Party Influences	-0.11	0.25	0.90	-0.17	0.25	0.84
Citizen & Officer Characteristics						
Indicators of Irrationality				-0.34	0.29	0.72
Citizen Age				0.17	0.12	1.19
Officer Minority				-0.22	0.38	0.80
Citizen Minority				-1.30*	0.41	0.27
Citizen Low Income				-0.72*	0.36	0.49
Model X^2	12.50	8 df		30.94*	13 df	
LLH Ratio X^2	0.20	1 df		18.43*	5 df	
Nagelkerke R^2	.06			.14		

* $p < .05$ two tailed test

Phase II Re-analysis

In terms of our phase II analysis strategy we are left with 79 cases total in which officers made a subsequent request for identification following the initial request. Previously we presented some selected bivariate relationships to illustrate the impact of commands, citizen income level, and race on the likelihood of complying with the second request. It is possible to generate a limited logistic model if one pools cases where a citizen was previously compliant with those who were previously non-compliant in phase I. Thus four independent variables can be entered in the model including previous level of compliance (1=complied, 0=non-compliant in phase I), whether police used commands in phase II (1=command, 0=else), and the minority status and income variables originally entered in phase I. The mean levels of each of these dummy variables is .34 for prior compliance, .04 for phase II commands, .77 for minority status, and .80 for low income status.

The model of phase II compliance (results not shown) indicates that the variables that predicted phase I compliance with requests for identification are not significant predictors of compliance in phase II of these encounters (model x^2=17.6, 4 d.f.). The model of phase II cooperation with police requests for identification is, however, better than chance because of the inclusion of the citizen's level of cooperation in phase I. Contrary to an expectation that cooperation or non-compliant positions would be maintained by a target citizen, we find the opposite. One's valence in phase I is reversed in phase II. This is plausible for several reasons. First, police who press compliant citizens with repeated questions concerning their identification may be perceived as illegitimate. Second, police may continue to press non-cooperative suspects for identification until they comply in a fashion similar to that reported by Sykes and Brent (1983). This conjecture on how citizens come to comply or rebel, however, indicates that continued exploration of these same questions, with more fine subdivisions of police-citizen encounters is warranted. In addition, the finding that race and class condition initial decisions to cooperate illustrates a need to understand the attitudes or values underlying that relationship. Anderson (1999) has proposed that the "code of the street" may make lower class minority youths in particular prone to defiance and non-cooperation with the police (e.g., Reisig and colleagues, 2003). Further exploration of the constellation of attitudes that engender such behavior when faced with an agent of the state is also required to better understand cooperation and rebellion in police-citizen encounters.

CONCLUSION

This chapter examined police requests for identification in 319, non-traffic, proactive street stops. For the most part coercive actions (excepting commands), procedurally just actions, and third party behavior had little impact on why citizens obeyed the initial requests for identification made by police. Minority and lower income status, were, however, both negatively related to cooperation with police requests for identification in this sample. This comports with research by Reisig, McCluskey, Mastrofski, and Terrill (2003) on citizen disrespect towards police. A concern with these findings is the need to establish what attitudes mediate the relationship between income level and minority status and decisions to thwart police authority. These findings beg further research to determine why these characteristics are linked to noncompliance, similar to Luckenbill and Doyle's (1989) argument for "disputatiousness" as an intermediate attitude that predicted aggression in lower class individuals. Thus we too must argue for further inquiry into how income and minority status link with citizen perceptions that ultimately generate higher levels of noncompliant behavior in these situations.

Our concern that requests for identification were theoretically distinct from requests for self-control appears to have some merit. The latter models are more heavily dependent on police behavior to explain compliance and, with respect to requests for identification we find that who is being asked is most important.

CHAPTER SEVEN

CONDITIONAL EFFECTS

This chapter focuses on variables that may condition the impact of our independent measures on citizen compliance. We analyze the impact of neighborhood distress, probable cause, the presence of an adversary, and citizen irrationality as important variables that may interact with our independent measures in predicting whether citizens comply. Our primary focus is on whether these condition the impact of procedural justice variables, but we will also attend to whether they condition other variables in the models. The effects of these four factors are addressed in the order of neighborhood distress, probable cause, presence of an adversary, and presence of irrational elements.

In chapter two we introduced the concept that the models of compliance might be conditioned by the presence or absence of these conditions. We first briefly revisit how these variables are expected to interact with the models of compliance. Concentrated disadvantage, since it has not been used in models previously, is given extensive treatment in this chapter. We anticipate that citizens encountered in more disadvantaged areas will attend less to procedurally just treatment than their counterparts in less disadvantaged neighborhoods. The presence of probable cause is likely to give police presence an overarching "legitimacy" thus increasing the effect of other procedurally just or unjust actions displayed by the police. The presence of an adversary is expected to transform the encounter into a contest for an outcome, thus increasing the importance of procedurally just action when compared to encounters where no adversary is present. Finally, in situations where citizens are operating under the influence of irrationality we expect that the effect of procedurally just action is diminished since the irrational citizen is less likely to attend to the "justice" in police actions when compared to his rational counterpart.

Since our measures have received ample treatment in chapters five and six we opt to briefly discuss them and quickly turn our attention to modeling compliance in each section. Previously we noted that three of the third party variables including the presence of a relative, the presence of a relative as adversary, and adversary presence were on the borderline of collinearity. Since we are arguing for including the presence of an adversary as an important conditional effect we will exclude two variables, presence of relatives and presence of relatives who are adversaries, since they would complicate analysis and would also likely be more problematic, in terms of collinearity, if included in split samples.[1] Each analysis will require splitting the sample on a dichotomous (or in the case of irrationality, a variable the indicates its absence) independent variable to assess differences across models. The indexes constructed in chapter five will be adopted as a mechanism to minimize the degrees of freedom used in the models. Finally, we restrict our attention to phase I requests for self-control as our dependent variable because of the limited number of cases in our sample of requests for identification and the limited number of phase II cases available.

NEIGHBORHOOD DISTRESS

The level of social distress in a neighborhood was previously noted as a factor that might condition how target citizens respond to police and situational stimuli. A variety of theoretical perspectives including control theory and strain theory focuses on the structural characteristics' effect on socialization (Hirschi, 1969; Merton, 1968). We argue that citizens in different areas have dissimilar conceptions of justified police action which would, in turn, indirectly affect the likelihood of citizen compliance (e.g., Gurr, 1971:26; Kerner, 1968:299-307). This hypothesis assumes that citizens' perceptions of tactics that police use to gain compliance are predicted by the social distress in the area. High levels of distress may not only affect the mean level of compliance (the intercept in models) but may also interact with our other independent measures. Below we introduce our measure of neighborhood distress and outline a strategy for assessing the impact of neighborhood distress on the likelihood of target compliance with requests for self-control.

Measuring Distress

Reisig and Parks (2001) have constructed an index of "concentrated disadvantage" which is consonant with the work of Sampson, Raudenbush, and Earls (1997). Measures from the 1990 census in the 98 neighborhoods in Indianapolis (N=50) and St. Petersburg (N=48) were used to create a factor score of concentrated disadvantage. The percent female headed households with children, percent minority, percent persons below poverty level, percent under age 18, and percent unemployed were used to create a weighted factor score (eigenvalue 3.47, factor loadings > .60). Table 7.1 presents the components of the factor scores, their factor loadings, and five example neighborhoods from the high distress, medium distress, and low distress areas in the two cities. By way of comparing distress across the five lowest distressed and five highest distressed neighborhoods we observe a percent unemployed ratio of 6.2:1 and percent below poverty ratio of 5.4:1.

In our sample of 939 police-suspect contacts that resulted in police requesting compliance, observers with the Project on Policing Neighborhoods recorded police-citizen contacts in 91 of the 98 neighborhoods. Complete data for this analysis were available in 904 cases, but 35 cases were missing data on the location of the encounter. We chose to subdivide our sample to compare models of citizen compliance in the most highly distressed areas with those in less distressed areas. The encounters occurring in the top quarter of the neighborhoods were considered to be "high distress" and the rest of the sample was used as a comparison. Hierarchical models were considered, but the dichotomous dependent variable and the small numbers of cases embedded in each neighborhood made those analyses untenable with the present data. Table 7.2 presents descriptive statistics for the 263 cases in the high distress areas and the 641 cases in the remainder of the two cities. Measures are identical to those presented in chapter five as are the indexes previously constructed in that chapter.

Table 7.1 Concentrated Disadvantage Measures at Selected Levels

Disadvantage Level	Percent Female Headed HH w/ Children	Percent Minority Residents	Percent Below Poverty	Percent Below 18 Years of Age	Percent Unemployed	Concentrated Disadvantage Index
Highest Five Neighborhoods	60.2	98.7	66.3	44.3	15.1	3.06
	30.1	97.6	53.0	41.6	13.5	1.92
	33.8	97.1	44.9	28.5	20.0	1.88
	41.0	90.8	37.8	35.5	12.3	1.66
	44.0	89.7	35.8	39.4	9.6	1.64
Middle Five Neighborhoods	4.1	51.5	40.7	14.1	8.3	-0.13
	14.2	67.4	8.8	27.1	7.2	-0.15
	13.2	2.6	22.2	27.5	10.5	-0.17
	19.1	18.3	22.1	23.2	7.4	-0.18
	14.9	28.4	13.3	30.0	8.1	-0.20
Lowest Five Neighborhoods	7.5	6.3	4.1	12.2	3.4	-1.32
	4.9	1.7	6.0	14.9	2.8	-1.35
	4.4	7.3	19.8	3.6	1.6	-1.37
	3.5	5.7	8.5	12.4	1.2	-1.45
	2.7	3.0	5.6	12.4	2.3	-1.49
Factor Loading	.928	.840	.882	.644	.841	

Table 7.2 Descriptive Statistics of Pooled Neighborhood Cases

	High Distress Neighborhoods (n=263)				All Other Neighborhoods (n=641)			
	Min.	Max.	Mean	S.D.	Min.	Max.	Mean	S.D.
Phase I Compliance	0	1	0.67	0.47	0	1	0.70	0.46
Independent Variables								
Police Entry	1	6	2.44	0.97	1	6	2.23	0.83
Procedural Justice Indicators								
Citizen Entry (Rectitude)	0	1	0.02	0.14	0	1	0.00	0.07
Citizen Entry (Morality)	0	1	0.03	0.17	0	1	0.02	0.14
Index of Ethicality	-1	2	0.38	0.77	-2	2	0.42	0.72
Index of Information Seeking	0	3	1.20	0.83	0	3	1.22	0.78
Index of Decision-Making	-1	1	0.18	0.47	-1	1	0.10	0.44
Probable Cause	0	1	0.63	0.48	0	1	0.53	0.50
Indicators of Police Coercion								
Police Mention Arrest	0	1	0.23	0.42	0	1	0.20	0.40
Index of Police Coercion	0	5	2.22	1.58	0	5	1.99	1.53
Citizen has Weapon	0	1	0.02	0.12	0	1	0.04	0.20
Police Present (sqrt)	0	3.46	0.32	0.57	0	2	0.23	0.48
Citizens Present (sqrt)	0	6.24	1.25	1.16	0	9.95	1.03	1.08
Gender Dyad	1	3	1.93	0.57	1	3	1.88	0.57
Third Party Influences								
Third Party Index	-2	2	0.10	0.66	-2	2	0.16	0.57
Adversary Present	0	1	0.32	0.47	0	1	0.32	0.47
Citizen/Officer Characteristics								
Indicators of Irrationality	0	3	0.56	0.70	0	3	0.60	0.73
Citizen Age	2	8	5.13	1.43	1	8	5.15	1.48
Officer Minority	0	1	0.32	0.47	0	1	0.15	0.36
Citizen Minority	0	1	0.86	0.34	0	1	0.53	0.50
Citizen Low Income	0	1	0.68	0.47	0	1	0.58	0.49

Concentrated Disadvantage and Models of Compliance

The dependent variable that we analyze is phase I compliance with police requests for self control. To analyze whether neighborhood distress level conditions our models of citizen compliance we estimated identical models including entry tactics, procedural justice indicators, coercion level, third party influences, and key citizen and officer characteristics for each set of cases, divided by neighborhood distress. Table 7.3 has the results of those two models as well as a z-score statistic that compares the impact of independent variables across models to determine whether the independent variable has a different impact depending upon the distress level (see Paternoster, Brame, Mazzerolle, and Piquero, 1998).

Table 7.3 Logistic Regression Analysis of Phase I Compliance by Neighborhood Distress Level

	High Distress Areas (n=263)			Other Areas (n=641)			Beta Comparison Statistic
	B	**S.E.**	**Exp(B)**	**B**	**S.E.**	**Exp(B)**	**ZSCORE**
Constant	-1.06	1.19	0.35	0.28	0.66	1.32	-0.98
Police Entry	0.01	0.19	1.01	-0.15	0.13	0.86	0.72
Procedural Justice							
Citizen Entry (Rectitude)	6.03	15.95	415.63	3.36	7.75	28.75	0.15
Citizen Entry (Morality)	-1.04	0.92	0.35	-0.47	0.67	0.62	-0.50
Index of Ethicality	-0.07	0.22	0.93	0.67*	0.16	1.96	-2.74[#]
Index of Information Seeking	0.66*	0.23	1.93	0.43*	0.14	1.54	0.85
Index of Decision-Making	0.29	0.38	1.34	0.75*	0.27	2.11	-0.98
Probable Cause	-0.48	0.36	0.62	-0.14	0.22	0.87	-0.81
Police Coercion							
Police Mention Arrest	0.64	0.43	1.89	0.51*	0.30	1.67	0.24
Index of Police Coercion	-0.09	0.12	0.91	0.02	0.08	1.02	-0.75
Citizen has Weapon	-0.08	1.36	0.92	0.85*	0.51	2.34	-0.65
Police Present (sqrt)	-0.08	0.28	0.92	-0.33	0.21	0.72	0.70
Citizens Present (sqrt)	-0.02	0.15	0.99	-0.03	0.10	0.97	0.08
Gender Dyad	0.03	0.29	1.03	-0.01	0.18	0.99	0.12
Third Party Influences							
Third Party Index	0.53*	0.26	1.69	0.82*	0.19	2.28	-0.92
Adversary Present	-0.76*	0.37	0.47	-0.25	0.23	0.78	-1.16

Characteristics	High Distress Areas (n=263)			Other Areas (n=641)			Beta Comparison Statistic
Indicators of Irrationality	-0.77*	0.25	0.46	-0.77*	0.15	0.46	-0.01
Citizen Age	0.33*	0.12	1.38	0.15*	0.07	1.16	1.24
Officer Minority	-0.18	0.36	0.83	-0.27	0.28	0.76	0.20
Citizen Minority	.0.71	0.47	2.02	-0.12	0.20	0.89	1.60
Citizen Low Income	-0.19	0.37	0.83	0.14	0.21	1.15	-0.76

Model x^2	75.79*	20 df	157.21* 20 df
Nagelkerke R^2	.35		.31

* $p < .05$ level, one-tailed test, # $p < .05$ level two-tailed test

At first blush it appears that our hypothesis that high levels of neighborhood distress may cancel positive effects of "fair" or "just" actions is supported. All three procedural justice indexes are significantly different from zero, and positively related to compliance in the less distressed neighborhoods. Only one procedural justice index is significant and positively related to compliance in the highly distressed neighborhood sample. It also appears that coercive power may behave differently across the two contexts since mentioning arrest yields compliance in less distressed neighborhoods but not in the highly distressed neighborhoods. Closer inspection and the use of a conservative statistical test (Paternoster et al., 1998) yield only one significantly different coefficient between the two models. In less distressed neighborhoods, ethical or respectful treatment is significantly more likely to generate compliant responses, holding all else constant, than when compared to high distress areas. One must be cautious in interpreting this finding, however, since there are 20 coefficients (and one intercept) compared and only one indicates a significant difference across models. Such a finding could be obtained by chance.

In terms of the individual model diagnostics, both have model chi-squares that are significant, indicating that the model fit in both instances is an improvement over chance (high distress model x^2=75.79, 20 d. f.; the less distressed neighborhoods x^2=157.21, 20 d. f.). There are four significant predictors of citizen compliance in distressed areas. For each one unit increase in the index of information seeking targets are nearly two times more likely to comply with the first police request for self-control. For every one unit increase in our index of third party influences the likelihood of compliance increases approximately 1.7 times, holding all else constant. Increases in the number of irrational elements reduce by half the likelihood of compliance, while one unit increases in citizen age increases compliance 1.4 times, holding everything else constant.

There are eight significant predictors of target compliance with requests for self-control in the less distressed neighborhoods. In the sample of cases from less distressed neighborhoods we find that all three indexes of procedural justice factors are significant predictors of citizen compliance. For every unit increase in the index of ethicality, target citizens are about two times more likely to comply. With every unit increase in the index of information seeking, target citizens are 1.5 times more likely to comply. For every unit increase in the index of decision-making, target citizens are more than two times more likely to comply. Two indicators of coercion are significant in the less distressed areas. If police mention arrest they are nearly 1.7 times more likely to gain compliance. Oddly, if a citizen has a weapon in the less distressed area they are 2.3 times more likely to comply with police requests for self control. With every one unit increase in our index of third party influences the likelihood of compliance increases approximately 2.3 times, holding all else constant. Increases in the number of irrational elements reduce by half the likelihood of compliance, while one unit increases in citizen age increase compliance nearly 1.2 times, holding everything else constant.

The findings are suggestive of similarities across neighborhoods; information seeking, third party actions, and the number of irrational elements affecting a citizen are significant predictors of compliance and cannot be ruled out as having identical impacts across the two models. These apparent consistencies seem contrary to our hypotheses that citizens would respond differently under similar stimuli. Given the findings from the z-score comparisons, we cannot conclude that the models are significantly different across neighborhoods.

One area where the present analysis falls short is in assigning neighborhood distress levels to the citizen. The mechanism for generating different responses to similar stimuli is likely environmental (e.g., Anderson, 1999) yet we naively assign citizens, who may not live in these neighborhoods, to the neighborhood of the police-target encounter. Ideally one would consider exposure to neighborhood distress as variable in terms of intensity and duration of an individual citizen's experience. Our model considers the transient visitor and lifetime resident encountered to be equally affected by the environment, which is a weak assumption. We are, thus, entering error into our neighborhood assignment of citizens, which is likely to influence our results. Regardless, the absence of substantial differences across models leads one to argue that neighborhood distress, as the setting or context within which an encounter occurs, has little impact on how targets weigh factors in making the decision to comply or rebel.

PROBABLE CAUSE

We theorized that probable cause to make an arrest might also change the dynamics of the police-target interaction. Citizens against whom police have no probable cause for arrest might be less inclined to weight procedural justice factors or coercive actions as levers that generate compliance. Conversely, just or fair action, combined with evidence rising to probable cause should increase the likelihood of compliance with police requests for self control.

Whether police had probable cause to arrest the citizen was measured as being present in phase I when the evidence level rises to two or more points from the following list (scores in parentheses): officer observes violation (2), officer obtains physical evidence implicating citizen (2), officer hears full confession (2), officer hears eyewitness testimony implicating citizen (1), officer hears partial confession (1). We split our sample on those cases where probable cause was present (n=529) and those where probable cause was not present (n=410) and descriptive measures for these two samples are presented in table 7.4.

Probable Cause and Models of Compliance

The dependent variable that we analyze is phase I compliance with police requests for self-control. To analyze the impact of the presence of probable cause on our models of citizen compliance we estimated

Table 7.4 Descriptive Statistics for Phase I Cases With and Without Probable Cause

	Probable Cause Present (n=529)				No Probable Cause Present (n=410)			
	Min.	**Max.**	**Mean**	**S.D.**	**Min.**	**Max.**	**Mean**	**S.D.**
Phase I Compliance	0	1	0.71	0.45	0	1	0.67	0.47
Independent Variables								
Police Entry	1	6	2.36	0.91	1	6	2.22	0.86
Procedural Justice								
Citizen Entry (Rectitude)	0	1	0.01	0.08	0	1	0.01	0.11
Citizen Entry (Morality)	0	1	0.02	0.14	0	1	0.03	0.16
Index of Ethicality	-2	2	0.40	0.74	-2	2	0.41	0.73
Index of Information Seeking	0	3	1.31	0.81	0	3	1.09	0.78
Index of Decision-Making	-1	1	0.23	0.46	-1	1	0.00	0.38
Police Coercion								
Police Mention Arrest	0	1	0.24	0.43	0	1	0.15	0.36
Index of Police Coercion	0	5	2.37	1.63	0	5	1.68	1.34
Citizen has Weapon	0	1	0.04	0.20	0	1	0.03	0.18
Police Present (sqrt)	0	3.46	0.24	0.51	0	1.73	0.28	0.50
Citizens Present (sqrt)	0	7	0.98	1	0	9.95	1.24	1.21
Gender Dyad	1	3	1.89	0.53	1	3	1.91	0.62
Third Party Influences								
Third Party Index	-2	2	0.16	0.57	-2	2	0.11	0.63
Adversary Present	0	1	0.21	0.41	0	1	0.46	0.50
Characteristics								
Indicators of Irrationality	0	3	0.53	0.70	0	3	0.63	0.75
Citizen Age	2	8	5.22	1.47	1	8	5.05	1.46
Officer Minority	0	1	0.19	0.39	0	1	0.23	0.42
Citizen Minority	0	1	0.63	0.48	0	1	0.61	0.49
Citizen Low Income	0	1	0.56	0.50	0	1	0.68	0.47

identical models across cases with probable cause and those without. Table 7.5 presents the results of those two models as well as a z-score statistic that compares the impact of independent variables across models.

The key element of these models is the comparison column in table 7.5. This presents the z-score statistic suggested by Paternoster et al., (1998) as a test for the significance of the differences in regression coefficients. Four contrasts appear to be significantly different across the models using a two-tail test, and one other will be discussed since it approaches significance and is theoretically interesting. The first to stand out is the intercept of the two models. This difference indicates that holding all other variables constant, the intercepts (the log-level of compliance) between models is significantly different. We can draw the inference that the target citizen in a situation where no probable cause exists is less likely to comply. This is contrary to our findings in chapter five, where probable cause, as a single predictor in the model did not attain statistical significance. The highest level of coercion that police use against citizens appears most important in those cases where the police have probable cause, where compliance is attenuated as greater levels of force are used against the target citizen. Such an effect is not found in cases where no probable cause is present and the z-statistic indicates the magnitude of difference is greater than would be expected by chance.

The audience effects on compliance vary substantially across the two samples. Citizens who are faced with a larger police audience, but who are asked to comply without probable cause are substantially less likely to comply than their counterparts against whom which probable cause exists. The converse is true of citizen effects, those citizens confronted with larger citizen audiences and no probable cause are more likely to comply than their counterparts against whom which probable cause for arrest is present. These two findings lead us to some post hoc explanations. First, increased police presence in the absence of probable cause aggravates those against whom no probable cause exists. The legitimacy of any police presence, much less an expansive one, is thrown into doubt and could become part of a target's calculus about the morality of police intervention.

Table 7.5 Probable Cause and Phase I Compliance: A Model Comparison

	Probable Cause Present (n=529)			No Probable Cause Present (n=410)			Beta Comparison Statistic
	B	**S.E.**	**Exp(B)**	**B**	**S.E.**	**Exp(B)**	**ZSCORE**
Constant	1.33*	0.75	3.80	-1.19	0.80	0.31	2.29[#]
Police Entry	-0.20	0.13	0.82	0.13	0.17	1.14	-1.54
Procedural Justice							
Citizen Entry (Rectitude)	4.85	12.73	128.28	5.01	9.40	149.97	-0.01
Citizen Entry (Morality)	-0.83	0.71	0.44	-0.18	0.79	0.84	-0.61
Index of Ethicality	0.32*	0.17	1.38	0.46*	0.19	1.58	-0.54
Index of Information	0.39*	0.15	1.48	0.57*	0.17	1.76	-0.76
Index of Decision-Making	0.75*	0.28	2.13	0.62*	0.34	1.86	0.30
Police Coercion							
Police Mention Arrest	0.21	0.29	1.24	1.07*	0.44	2.91	-1.62
Index of Police Coercion	-0.16*	0.08	0.86	0.15	0.11	1.16	-2.18[#]
Citizen has Weapon	0.48	0.56	1.62	0.50	0.76	1.64	-0.02
Police Present (sqrt)	0.04	0.23	1.04	-0.63*	0.26	0.53	1.96[#]
Citizens Present (sqrt)	-0.19	0.13	0.83	0.16	0.11	1.17	-2.03[#]
Gender Dyad	0.00	0.22	1.00	-0.07	0.20	0.93	0.23
Third Party Influences							
Third Party Index	0.46*	0.20	1.59	1.05*	0.23	2.85	-1.91
Adversary Present	-0.48*	0.28	0.62	-0.05	0.27	0.95	-1.10
Characteristics							
Indicators of Irrationality	-0.77*	0.17	0.46	-0.80*	0.18	0.45	0.13
Citizen Age	0.09	0.08	1.09	0.25*	0.09	1.28	-1.31
Officer Minority	-0.19	0.30	0.83	-0.27	0.30	0.76	0.19
Citizen Minority	-0.03	0.24	0.97	-0.22	0.26	0.80	0.55
Citizen Low Income	-0.01	0.24	0.99	0.11	0.27	1.11	-0.32
Model x^2	130.33*	19 df		115.27*	19 df		
Nagelkerke R^2	.31			.34			

* $p < .05$ one-tailed test, # $p < .05$ two-tailed test

With respect to citizen audience, citizens who are confronted with a larger audience presence, and against whom evidence rises to that of probable cause, thus suffer from a disintegrative shaming situation where non-compliance may be a knee-jerk response. This is, of course, post hoc theorizing, and not a tested hypothesis.

Finally, the third party influences, though statistically significant in both models, are far larger than would be had by chance in the models of compliance targets against whom which probable cause has not been generated. We used a two tail test for the z-score comparisons, therefore the difference is not highlighted as statistically significant, but we consider the magnitude of the difference between coefficients as sufficient to warrant discussion. That third parties matter more where legitimacy is lacking (i.e. there is no probable cause) comports with prior theorizing about third party influences. If we take as a premise that probable cause establishes a baseline for legitimacy, then the power of third party influences would be expected to vary across situations depending upon the presence or absence of probable cause. This follows from that premise; since the third party's relative standing to the authority figure (in these cases a police officer asking the target citizen to exercise self-control) is diminished in those cases where prima facie legitimacy, in the form of probable cause, has been established.

In cases where probable cause is present prior to the request for self control the model chi-square is significant (x^2=130.33, 19 d. f.). The index of ethicality is significantly different from zero, and holding all else constant, a one unit increase in that measure increases the odds of compliance 1.4 times. The index of information seeking is also statistically significant and indicates that for every one unit increase in that measure the odds of compliance increase 1.5 times. The index of decision-making is statistically significant and increases the odds of compliance more than 2 times for every one unit increase in that measure. The index of coercion is statistically significant, and for every one unit increase it increases the odds of non-compliance almost 1.2 times. The third party index is a significant predictor of target citizen's decisions to comply and for every unit increase in that measure the likelihood of compliance increases slightly more than 1.5 times. Finally, increases in the number of irrational elements affecting a target reduce the likelihood of compliance, holding all else constant, by half.

The model that we fitted to the cases without probable cause present in phase I indicates a better than chance fit, as evidenced by a significant chi-square statistic (x^2=115.27, 19 d.f.). Closer examination of the models indicates that the three indexes of procedurally just actions are all significant and positive. Holding all else constant a one unit increase in ethicality yields nearly 1.6 times increase in the odds of compliance, a one unit increase in the information index yields nearly a 1.8 times increase in the odds of compliance, and a one unit increase in the decision-making index yields nearly a 1.9 times increase in the odds of compliance.

Two indicators of coercion affect targets' likelihood of compliance with requests for self-control in cases where probable cause is not present. If police mention arrest then the odds of compliance increase 2.9 times. For every unit increase in the transformed measure of police presence the likelihood of compliance is halved. In terms of third party influences, a one unit increase in that index generates nearly a 2.9 times increase in the odds of compliance, holding all else constant.

Two citizen characteristics are significant predictors of citizen compliance in cases where probable cause is not present. As the number of irrational elements increase by one unit, the odds of compliance are reduced by more than half. As citizen age increases by one unit the odds of compliance increases by 1.3, holding all else constant.

We conclude that the presence or absence of probable cause does substantially impact the factors that predict citizen compliance. Our analysis indicates that police and citizen audience effects and the police's highest level of coercion generate substantial differences in citizens' decisions to comply, contingent upon the presence or absence of probable cause. Since probable cause must figure into a calculus made by the target citizens these models probably underestimate its true effect on decision-making. This is likely true since targets are probably not always aware of whether probable cause has been generated against them, or not, and therefore our objective measure (inasmuch as it is coded from a narrative written by a disinterested third party) is an imprecise measure their perception of probable cause.

THE ADVERSARY

We theorized that the presence of an adversary may condition the dynamics of the police-target interaction. Citizens in an adversarial contest may be inclined to grant greater weight to procedural justice factors and less to coercive actions as levers that generate compliance. In particular, the concern for a fair outcome would increase citizens' focus on the actions of police as they render a quasi-judicial verdict in the adversarial setting. Tyler (1990) has suggested that the importance of different procedural justice elements is conditioned by context. Hence we should observe differences across models where adversaries are present and where police are acting as arbitrators compared to those situations where no adversary is present and police are relying on statutory or legal power to render a verdict. As with previous analyses we split our sample on those cases where an adversary was present (n=299) and those where an adversary was not present (n=640) and descriptive measures for these two samples are presented in table 7.6.

Adversary Presence and Models of Compliance

To analyze the effect of the presence of an adversary on models of citizen compliance we estimated identical models on the split sample. Table 7.7 has the results of those two models as well as a z-score statistic comparing the effects of independent variables across models. The individual models present a vehicle for comparing cases where adversaries are present to those where no adversaries are present. The z-score comparison statistic is presented in the final column of table 7.7. Only two contrasts appear to be significantly different across the models. In cases where no adversary is present, the index of decision-making is more likely to influence the decision to comply. This is congruent with Tyler's (1990) assertion that the importance of procedural factors will vary across settings. In his research he was inclined to differentiate between administrative decisions, police decisions, and judicial decisions. Here we have differentiated two contexts that the same authority (police) encounters and delivers quasi-judicial verdicts. Evidence of sound decision-making, as we have operationalized it, appears to most strongly influence citizen compliance when the citizen is in a situation where the police are relying on statutory/legal authority as opposed to intervention in a dispute. This finding is, however, contrary to our stated expectations.

Table 7.6 Descriptive Statistics for Phase I Cases With and Without Adversaries

	Adversary Present (n=299)				No Adversary (n=640)			
	Min.	Max	Mean	S.D.	Min.	Max	Mean	S.D.
Phase I Compliance	0.00	1.00	0.58	0.49	0.00	1.00	0.75	0.44
Independent Variables								
Police Entry	1.00	6.00	2.19	0.93	1.00	6.00	2.35	0.86
Procedural Justice								
Citizen Entry (Rectitude)	0.00	1.00	0.02	0.13	0.00	1.00	0.00	0.07
Citizen Entry (Morality)	0.00	1.00	0.02	0.13	0.00	1.00	0.03	0.16
Index of Ethicality	-1.00	2.00	0.46	0.77	-2.00	2.00	0.38	0.72
Index of Information	0.00	3.00	1.05	0.75	0.00	3.00	1.29	0.82
Index of Decision-Making	-1.00	1.00	0.00	0.47	-1.00	1.00	0.19	0.42
Police have Probable Cause	0.00	1.00	0.37	0.48	0.00	1.00	0.65	0.48
Police Coercion								
Police Mention Arrest	0.00	1.00	0.17	0.37	0.00	1.00	0.22	0.41
Index of Police Coercion	0.00	5.00	1.76	1.42	0.00	5.00	2.21	1.59
Citizen has Weapon	0.00	1.00	0.05	0.22	0.00	1.00	0.03	0.17
Police Present (sqrt)	0.00	1.73	0.31	0.53	0.00	3.46	0.23	0.49
Citizens Present (sqrt)	0.00	7.00	1.30	1.02	0.00	9.95	1.00	1.13
Gender Dyad	1.00	3.00	1.84	0.58	1.00	3.00	1.93	0.56
Third Party Influences								
Third Party Index	-1.00	2.00	0.11	0.58	-2.00	2.00	0.15	0.60
Characteristics								
Citizen Age	0.00	3.00	0.89	0.79	0.00	3.00	0.43	0.64
Officer Minority	1.00	8.00	5.10	1.53	2.00	8.00	5.16	1.43
Citizen Minority	0.00	1.00	0.24	0.43	0.00	1.00	0.19	0.39
Citizen Low Income	0.00	1.00	0.64	0.48	0.00	1.00	0.61	0.49

Table 7.7 The Presence and Absence of Adversaries: The Effect on Compliance

	Adversary (n=299)			No Adversary (n=640)			Comparison Statistic
	B	**S.E.**	**Exp(B)**	**B**	**S.E.**	**Exp(B)**	**ZSCORE**
Constant	-0.90	0.81	0.41	0.40	0.70	1.49	-1.21
Police Entry	0.03	0.16	1.03	-0.11	0.13	0.90	0.70
Procedural Justice							
Citizen Entry (Rectitude)	6.03	15.96	417.43	5.54	12.35	253.48	0.02
Citizen Entry (Morality)	-0.63	1.07	0.53	-0.44	0.60	0.64	-0.16
Index of Ethicality	0.33*	0.19	1.39	0.39*	0.16	1.48	-0.23
Index of Information	0.59*	0.20	1.81	0.40*	0.14	1.50	0.77
Index of Decision-Making	0.10	0.29	1.10	1.23*	0.35	3.41	-2.46[#]
Police have Probable Cause	-0.46	0.31	0.63	-0.14	0.23	0.87	-0.86
Police Coercion							
Police Mention Arrest	0.34	0.37	1.40	0.57*	0.31	1.76	-0.48
Index of Police Coercion	-0.08	0.12	0.92	-0.02	0.08	0.98	-0.45
Citizen has Weapon	1.19*	0.67	3.27	0.32	0.60	1.38	0.96
Police Present (sqrt)	-0.10	0.26	0.91	-0.34	0.22	0.71	0.72
Citizens Present (sqrt)	0.04	0.14	1.04	-0.02	0.10	0.98	0.30
Gender Dyad	-0.02	0.23	0.98	0.01	0.19	1.01	-0.08
Third Party Influences							
Third Party Index	1.01*	0.26	2.76	0.63*	0.18	1.87	1.22
Characteristics							
Indicators of Irrationality	-0.38*	0.18	0.68	-0.97*	0.17	0.38	2.43[#]
Citizen Age	0.17*	0.09	1.19	0.18*	0.08	1.20	-0.04
Officer Minority	-0.46	0.32	0.63	-0.05	0.27	0.95	-0.98
Citizen Minority	0.02	0.28	1.02	-0.19	0.22	0.83	0.56
Citizen Low Income	0.18	0.29	1.20	-0.05	0.23	0.95	0.62
Model x^2	58.87*	19 df		152.83*	19 df		
Nagelkerke R^2	.24			.31			

The second effect that we observe is that the irrational citizen is likely to be more rebellious in encounters without adversaries. This seems curious since preexisting disputes would seem to contain the potential for more serious rebellion when coupled with irrationality. One explanation could be that our sample is censored inasmuch as police may remove the most irrational party from a dispute through arrest, rather than attempt an informal solution, to defuse potential conflict. This would remove those who are extremely irrational from that sample and bias our results.

In cases where an adversary is present prior to the request for self control the model chi-square is significant (x^2=58.87, 19 d. f.). The index of ethicality is significantly different from zero, and holding all else constant, a one unit increase in that measure increases the odds of compliance 1.4 times. The index of information seeking is also statistically significant and indicates that for every one unit increase in that measure the odds of compliance increase 1.8 times. Whether a citizen has a weapon is statistically significant, and in instances where a target had a weapon it increased the odds of compliance more than 3 times.

The third party index is a significant predictor of target citizen's decisions to comply and for every unit increase in that measure the likelihood of compliance increases nearly 2.8 times. The number of irrational elements affecting a target reduces the likelihood of compliance 1.5 times, holding all else constant, for each one unit increase in that measure. Finally, for every unit increase in age, the likelihood of compliance increases approximately 1.2 times.

The model that we fitted to the cases without adversaries present in phase I indicates a better than chance fit, as evidenced by a significant chi-square statistic (x^2=152.83, 19 d.f.). Closer examination of the models indicates that the three indexes of procedurally just actions are all significant and positive. Holding all else constant a one unit increase in ethicality yields nearly 1.5 times increase in the odds of compliance, a one unit increase in the information index yields a 1.5 times increase in the odds of compliance, and a one unit increase in the decision-making index yields a 3.4 times increase in the odds of compliance. If the police mentioned arrest in cases with no adversary present then the odds of compliance were increased nearly 1.8 times.

The third party index is a significant predictor of target citizen's decisions to comply. For every unit increase in that measure the likelihood of compliance increases nearly 1.9 times. The number of irrational elements affecting a target reduces the likelihood of compliance 2.6 times for each one unit increase in that measure. Finally, for every unit increase in age, the likelihood of compliance increases approximately 1.2 times.

Overall, these results indicate that the presence of an adversary does not substantially affect the factors that predict citizen compliance. Despite our interpretation of the differences across models, we must note that there are 20 coefficients compared across models and only two reached the level of statistical significance. Such findings could be the result of chance and lend to the interpretation that citizens attend to similar factors in these two types of police-citizen encounters when calculating a decision to comply.

IRRATIONALITY

The presence of strong emotion, mental illness, or evidence of alcohol or drug use has been consistently and negatively related to citizen compliance in the various models presented in this study. Here we propose that beyond the direct effect that these irrational elements provide, they may also interact with other independent measures. In particular, since our procedural justice measures are reliant on the formation of a perception of just or fair action, those citizens affected by irrationality may be less likely to attend to police tactics as when compared to their sober, sane, and calm peers.

Thus we propose subdividing our sample into those with no indication of irrationality in phase I and compare them to those who have at least one element of irrationality (mental illness, obvious physical effects from alcohol or drug use, or elevated emotions). Similar to previous analyses presented in this chapter we split our sample on those cases no irrational elements were present (n=516) and those where at least one element was present (n=423) and descriptive measures for these two samples are presented in table 7.8.

Table 7.8 Descriptive Statistics on Cases Where Irrational
Elements Are/Are Not Present

	Citizen not Affected by Irrational Elements (n=516)				Citizen Affected by Irrational Elements (n=423)			
	Min.	Max.	Mean	S.D.	Min.	Max.	Mean	S.D.
Phase I Compliance	0	1	0.82	0.38	0	1	0.54	0.50
Independent Variables								
Police Entry	1	5	2.18	0.65	1	6	2.44	1.09
Procedural Justice								
Citizen Entry (Rectitude)	0	1	0.01	0.10	0	1	0.01	0.08
Citizen Entry (Morality)	0	1	0.01	0.11	0	1	0.04	0.19
Index of Ethicality	-1	2	0.44	0.69	-2	2	0.37	0.79
Index of Information	0	3	1.36	0.76	0	3	1.04	0.82
Index of Decision-Making	-1	1	0.17	0.47	-1	1	0.07	0.41
Police have Probable Cause	0	1	0.59	0.49	0	1	0.53	0.50
Police Coercion								
Police Mention Arrest	0	1	0.19	0.40	0	1	0.21	0.41
Index of Police Coercion	0	5	1.98	1.59	0	5	2.16	1.49
Citizen has Weapon	0	1	0.03	0.17	0	1	0.04	0.20
Police Present (sqrt)	0	3.46	0.24	0.49	0	2.24	0.28	0.53
Citizens Present (sqrt)	0	9.95	1.05	1.14	0	7	1.15	1.05
Gender Dyad	1	3	1.94	0.55	1	3	1.85	0.60
Third Party Influences								
Third Party Index	-2	2	0.20	0.57	-2	2	0.06	0.61
Adversary Present	0	1	0.20	0.40	0	1	0.46	0.50
Characteristics								
Citizen Age	1	8	4.97	1.48	2	8	5.36	1.42
Officer Minority	0	1	0.21	0.41	0	1	0.20	0.40
Citizen Minority	0	1	0.63	0.48	0	1	0.62	0.49
Citizen Low Income	0	1	0.55	0.50	0	1	0.68	0.47

Irrationality and Models of Compliance

To analyze the effect of the presence of irrationality on models of citizen compliance we once again estimated identical models for the two samples. Table 7.9 presents the results of those two models as well as a z-score statistic that comparing the effects of independent variables across models.

These two models present a vehicle to compare cases in which targets are affected by irrationality to those in which, at least by neutral observer's standards, citizens are rational. The z-score measure is presented in the final column of table 7.9. Three contrasts appear to be significantly different across the models. The index of ethicality, the effect of third parties, and the presence of minority lead officers are significantly different across the two samples.

In cases where officers exhibit greater ethicality and are more accommodating of citizen's needs irrational citizens respond more readily by exhibiting compliance than their sober, sane, and calm counterparts. The rational citizen is also more likely to be influenced by a model on scene than the irrational citizen who is asked for self-control. Conversely, the sober, sane, and calm rational citizen is significantly less likely to acquiesce to the request for self-control that is given by a minority officer. This could be a residue of similar race effects that Mastrofski, Snipes, and Supina (1996) found in the Richmond study. The fact that this difference emerges when the sample is divided on irrationality requires further exploration. Beyond the caveat that two differences in twenty comparisons may be chance, we also can look to the distribution on the dependent variable across samples as a possible factor.

The irrational sample has 46 percent non-compliance and the rational sample has only eighteen percent non-compliance. Further examination of contingency tables of officer race by citizen compliance indicates that, in instances of encounters with irrational citizens the distributions of compliance are identical across officer race. Comparing officer race and compliance of rational targets we find that in sixteen percent of the cases citizens rebelled against white officers, but in nearly 27 percent of the cases rational citizens rebelled against minority officers. In a previous section we argued that citizens (not just rational citizens) would be more likely to rebel against minority officers, and it appears that the comparison of these coefficients support that, but only in cases where citizens are unaffected by mental illness, strong emotion, or alcohol.

Table 7.9 The Presence and Absence of Irrational Elements: The Impact on Compliance

	Citizen not Affected by Irrational Elements (n=516)			Citizen Affected by Irrational Elements (n=423)			Beta Comparison Statistic
	B	**S.E.**	**Exp(B)**	**B**	**S.E.**	**Exp(B)**	**ZSCORE**
Constant	0.51	0.94	1.66	-0.95	0.70	0.39	1.25
Police Entry	-0.18	0.22	0.83	-0.06	0.12	0.94	-0.48
Procedural Justice							
Citizen Entry (Rectitude)	4.89	9.58	132.35	5.65	12.43	282.95	-0.05
Citizen Entry (Morality)	-0.46	1.08	0.63	-0.46	0.58	0.63	0.00
Index of Ethicality	0.04	0.20	1.04	0.57*	0.15	1.76	-2.12[#]
Index of Information	0.51*	0.18	1.67	0.41*	0.15	1.51	0.43
Index of Decision-Making	0.86*	0.33	2.37	0.26	0.28	1.30	1.39
Police have Probable Cause	-0.02	0.29	0.98	-0.25	0.24	0.78	0.61
Police Coercion							
Police Mention Arrest	0.58	0.42	1.78	0.55*	0.30	1.73	0.06
Index of Police Coercion	0.02	0.10	1.02	-0.06	0.09	0.95	0.59
Citizen has Weapon	-0.24	0.67	0.78	1.02*	0.59	2.78	-1.41
Police Present (sqrt)	0.06	0.28	1.06	-0.52*	0.22	0.59	1.63
Citizens Present (sqrt)	-0.08	0.12	0.92	-0.03	0.11	0.97	-0.31
Gender Dyad	0.19	0.23	1.21	-0.08	0.19	0.92	0.91
Third Party Influences							
Third Party Index	1.20*	0.26	3.32	0.50*	0.19	1.64	2.17[#]
Adversary Present	-0.59*	0.32	0.55	-0.32	0.24	0.72	-0.67
Characteristics							
Citizen Age	0.11	0.09	1.12	0.22*	0.08	1.24	-0.91
Officer Minority	-0.76*	0.29	0.47	0.26	0.29	1.30	-2.49[#]
Citizen Minority	-0.24	0.28	0.79	0.04	0.23	1.04	-0.77
Citizen Low Income	0.16	0.27	1.17	-0.08	0.24	0.93	0.66
Model x^2	81.25*	19 df		81.98*	19 df		
Nagelkerke R^2	.24			.24			

* $p < .05$ one-tailed test, # $p < .05$ two-tailed test

The model fitted to the cases where irrational elements are present in phase I indicates a better than chance fit, as evidenced by a significant chi-square statistic (x^2=81.98, 19 d.f.). The index of ethicality and the index of information seeking both have coefficients that are significantly different from zero. Holding all else constant a one unit increase in ethicality yields nearly 1.8 times increase in the odds of compliance, and a one unit increase in the information index yields a 1.5 times increase in the odds of compliance.

Three indicators of coercion have coefficients that are significantly different from zero. If the police mentioned arrest in cases where targets are affected by irrational elements then the odds of compliance were increased 1.7 times (which seems to dispute the notion that irrational targets do not pay attention to consequences). Irrational citizens with weapons are nearly 2.8 times more likely to comply than their unarmed counterparts. A one unit increase in the number of police present reduces the likelihood of compliance 1.7 times. With respect to the influence of third parties on the irrational target, the coefficient for the index is significantly different from zero. The odds ratio for the third party index indicates that for every unit increase in that measure the likelihood of compliance increases 1.6 times. Finally, for every unit increase in age, the likelihood of compliance increases approximately 1.2 times.

In cases where no elements of irrationality are present prior to the request for self control the model chi-square is significant (x^2=81.25, 19 d. f.). The index of information seeking is statistically significant and indicates that for every one unit increase in that measure the odds of compliance increase nearly 1.7 times. The index of decision-making is significantly different from zero, and holding all else constant, a one unit increase in that measure increases the odds of compliance nearly 2.4 times. The index of ethicality is not significantly different from zero for those not affected by any irrational elements.

Both third party coefficients are significantly different from zero. The third party index is a significant predictor of target citizen's decisions to comply, and for every unit increase in that measure the likelihood of compliance increases 3.3 times. The presence of an adversary reduces the likelihood of compliance by nearly half, holding all else constant. Interestingly, rational citizens, holding all else constant, are half as likely to obey a request for self-control from a minority officer compared to their white counterparts.

Overall, the results indicate that the presence of irrationality does condition some factors that predict citizen compliance. It appears that the irrational citizen is more readily pushed to rebellion by disrespect or coaxed to compliance by magnanimous treatment when compared with the rational citizen. This is contrary to our stated hypothesis, in which we argued that the irrational would have diminished capacity to process the justice or injustice of police actions. The rational citizen, on the other hand, appears to attend to what other citizens are doing on scene as a cue for his or her behavior, and also interprets the characteristics of the officer as a cue for determining whether he or she should comply.

CONCLUSION

We have examined four conditional models of citizen compliance. Two have produced only one or two significant interactions. From these we conclude that the character of the neighborhood in which citizens encounter the police have little impact on their decision to comply when contrasted with the more immediate stimuli presented by the police. Similarly, it appears that, for the most part, citizens are influenced by similar factors in deciding to comply regardless of the presence or absence of an adversary.

Within the models for probable cause we found the greatest divergence, which was concentrated largely in the domain of police coercion. The index of coercion was negatively associated with compliance for targets in situations with probable cause present. This is consonant with the findings of Paternoster et al. (1997) indicating that less forceful tactics might be more successful in obtaining suspect compliance. In their analyses the handcuffing of citizens was considered a procedural affront, and perhaps in cases where probable cause exists, greater coercion promotes, rather than quells rebellion.

Similarly, the rational citizen appears to attend to who is making the request and how others are behaving on the scene more than the irrational citizens. The irrational citizens, conversely, are more likely to respond to how they are treated, in terms of respect, when compared with rational citizens.

The four sets of analyses give us caution with regard to interpreting models presented in chapter five. There are interactive effects in each of the models of compliance that we estimated. This may, therefore, require further theorizing with regard to other aspects of police-citizen encounters that may provide different "contexts" for interpreting the actions of authorities. For instance, the mobilization (proactive or reactive) may also condition how citizens respond to requests for self control. One could also imagine that the type of problem that police and citizens are negotiating over is a similar "contextual" factor that might condition the effects of police actions on citizen compliance. Taken as a whole, however, there appears to be more similarity than difference across all the models. Overall we made 80 comparisons of coefficients and found nine that were statistically different across the models (intercepts excluded), a rate of eleven percent. From a different perspective 71 of 80 comparisons could not be discerned as statistically different from zero, so nearly 90 percent of the comparisons failed to reject the null hypothesis.[2]

CHAPTER EIGHT

CONCLUSIONS AND FUTURE RESEARCH

"O, it is excellent
To have a giant's strength!
But it is tyrannous
To use it like a giant."
William Shakespeare, *Measure for Measure*

This conclusion has several aims. First we intend to place this research in a broader framework of human behavior and interaction. Second we will attend to the major theoretical domains that have been outlined as important for explaining compliance. Third we will briefly review some key findings and how these findings relate back to the theoretical foundations upon which this research has been built. Finally we will put this research in context as a commencement for future research.

Our research has explored a fundamental question in the social sciences (see Gibbs, 1989, who might recast this as an issue of control): Why do targets comply with requests? The phenomenon is ubiquitous across human interactions. Parents ask for compliance, countries seek compliance, organizations require employee compliance, and police ask for citizen compliance. The latter has been the narrow framework from which we have explored this larger question.

At the outset of this study we noted four dimensions of compliance situations that should be considered when trying to understand why targets comply. Police citizen interactions in face to face encounters were determined to be unique when compared on these dimensions with other compliance situations. These situations studied herein occur in close proximity (as opposed to bureaucracies such as the IRS dealing with clients such as taxpayers) which makes the face to face study of micro-level interactions feasible. Police, in the context of police-citizen encounters, were described as being reliant on coercive power bases to gain compliance (e.g., Bittner 1970) as compared with doctors who can exercise expert power when making requests of patients. The relationship between the target and the requestor is transient and likely to exist only for the interaction period, which is much different from the relationship and interaction routines one might find in studying parents and children. Finally, the admission status of the target, in these interactions, is likely to be involuntary. These differences led us to consider the generation of theoretical statements that might best fit the dynamics of the police-citizen encounter.

At the core of that theoretical exercise was reconciling two images of humans. First, we considered people to be avoiders of pain. In that sense the coercive power that police bring to bear on a situation should influence the likelihood of compliance. Second, we considered humans to be seekers of justice. As such we made the tactics of police that comport with "just" and "fair" action (or unjust, or unfair action) a central component of our models.

A SUMMARY OF FINDINGS

The models we produced tell two stories. One involves identification requests in proactive street stops. Here we find little predictable about who complies. Regardless of police actions obedience to authority is near universal. Perhaps the identification requests are perceived as legitimate information seeking by the police. The simple assumption that citizens comply with that type of request would be right in nearly 80 percent of the phase I cases, and 88 percent of the cases where police asked non-compliant citizens for licenses or identification a second time. Of the 319 citizens involved in proactive street stops, only 21, or about seven percent, maintained their noncompliant position.

The interpretation of those results, in light of the weak explanatory models, is that identification requests are perceived as within the universe of legitimate police requests, even in proactive street stops. This comports with Milgram's research suggesting compliance is obtained when the target is placed in a situation where the request is legitimate. Alternatively, we could conclude that people comply with these requests because they comport with the expectation that police seek information. That is post hoc theorizing, but it is supported by the fact that police seeking information in our other analyses increase the likelihood of gaining compliance. Perhaps information seeking demonstrates commitment to larger principles of justice, as our theorizing proposes.

Our primary dependent variable, police requests for self-control will serve as the focal point for the remainder of our conclusions. It is distinguished from a request for identification in that it represents a "verdict" delivered to the target citizen as a solution to the problem at hand. The findings in predicting compliance with those requests helps inform us about police acting as quasi-judicial functionaries and in a very common, albeit, informal role within society (e.g. Bayley, 1986). This is especially important in understanding how citizens respond to informal intervention in their lives, by formal agents of the state, which according to recent research (Bureau of Justice Statistics, 2001) is most common, with more than ten percent of the adult population reporting involvement in traffic stops.

To some extent that perspective for examining the compliance question has directed us at three very specific theoretical traditions. First we explored procedural justice, in micro-processual context of police-citizen encounters. Second we addressed coercion which Westley (1970), Bittner (1970), and Skolnick (1966) found to be so central to the police role and social psychologists (Tedeschi and Felson 1994) consider vital in understanding compliance. Finally, the significance of third parties and the tenor of their actions have been suggested by Milgram (1973) as an important sensitizing component to our understanding of citizen obedience in police-citizen encounters.

The cautions of Mastrofski (1999) about the quality of police work and how people are treated resonates with our findings. As police seek more information from citizens they become more likely to comply. Police respect enhances compliance, and police disrespect diminishes compliance. Police noting their decisions are rooted in leniency or legal considerations also enhances the likelihood of compliance.

Coercion is not as central to obedience, at least in police-citizen encounters where compliance is sought, as social interactionists might predict (Tedeschi and Felson, 1994 for example). Mentioning arrest, appears to be inconsistent at best in driving citizens towards obedience, but no other coercive act such as handcuffing, arresting, or threatening appears to persuade citizens to comply or rebel. Though based on smaller numbers of cases, our analyses of follow-up requests for self-control indicated that our index of coercion significantly reduced citizen compliance. The fact that coercion does not promote rebellion among those initially asked for compliance is important, but this research also indicates that coercion applied to citizens against whom which compliance requests are repeated is not effective in generating the desired results.

THEORETICAL IMPORTANCE

Just treatment, as we have considered information seeking, respectful treatment, and decision quality/impartiality, do promote compliance in police citizen encounters. This is interesting from two theoretical perspectives. First, the tradition of procedural justice research as it moved from psychological responses (Thibaut and Walker, 1975; Tyler and Folger, 1980) to behavioral responses (McEwen and Maiman, 1984; Tyler, 1990) has predicted that normative features of authority behavior matter. We find they are extremely powerful (relative to other domains) in explaining obedience to police requests for self control. Further research that can establish the linkage between specific police actions and citizen perceptions is necessary, since we have made assumptions about the linkage in this research.

The second theoretical tradition that is illuminated by this research is police research itself. Coercion has long been a central notion in understanding police work (Paoline, 2003; Bittner, 1970; Westley, 1970; Skolnick, 1966). Alternative conceptions of "what police do" has relied on eloquence (Muir, 1977: 227) and repetitive verbalization (Sykes and Brent, 1980) to explain routine interaction with citizens. We argued, from this tradition, that police power is rooted in coercion, but noted in our development of a theory of compliance that eloquence and interaction could play important roles in influencing citizens.

Our findings make us wonder if coercive power bases have been supplanted by legitimate power bases. Police may represent the "iron fist in the velvet glove," but this research develops a picture of police success based on increasing reliance on legitimate authority. If our assumptions about police actions building a sense of justice in their clientele are correct, then police are gaining acquiescence not from coercion but from authority that is perceived as legitimate. The vast numbers of encounters that include no force or legal sanctions attest to a new picture of policing. An alternative interpretation is that the coercive authority wielded by police establishes a base level of compliance merely through presence and its potential use.

Skolnick (1966) and Bittner (1970) commented on policing at a time when there were open challenges to authority and active questioning of the legitimacy of societal institutions. That they observed the importance of coercion as the power base of policing is not surprising given the circumstances. The present research indicates that citizens comply when they are confronted with an authority that is providing stimuli that, arguably, provoke a sense of just action. Citizens also respond to police in accordance with third parties on the scene. Citizens appear to attend little to the amount of verbal, physical, or legal coercion police bring to bear when requesting self-control. The importance of the self-presentation of police, illustrates the prescience of Muir (1977:227), who argued that eloquence was a fundamental component of "professional" police. Coupled with the work of Sykes and Brent (1980) we argue that the control of situations, through the seeking of citizen self-control, is reliant on language skills and tactical scripts that give citizens a sense that police are engaged in legitimate action.

Though coercion may be a central component of the police role, it appears to serve little to enhance compliance when first asked or when requests are repeated by the police. The snapshots of police-citizen interactions that we have used as data, like the work of Tyler (1990; 2001) and others, appears to have developed into a picture of citizens as "seekers of justice."

Finally, we must look backward at how the setting of this research (face to face encounters between citizens and police as compared with other instances where authorities request compliance) may produce research that diverges from findings in other settings with regard to the four dimensions that we have used to characterize authority and target relationships. These are offered as testable hypotheses derived from the present research results. As proximity between authority and target increases, the importance of procedurally just actions is likely to be diminished. We surmise this because interactions are likely to routinized through forms, as might be the case with much of the IRS's oversight of taxpayer compliance. In situations that are less transient, it is conceivable that the importance of procedurally just action may be heightened. Regular interaction is likely to generate expectations of how an authority ought to behave. The coercive power base of police authority might also indicate that as one moves to settings where other power bases are emphasized, the importance of fair and just procedures might be attenuated. Lastly, we argue that in situations where admission status is involuntary, the importance of justice and fairness concerns will be higher when compared with situations where admission is voluntary.

FUTURE RESEARCH

Future research on compliance needs to explore the specific police actions that develop a "sense of justice" or "sense of injustice" among citizens encountered by police. That research also needs to explore how preexisting attitudes affect the interpretation of police actions during encounters. The present research is based on the assumption that the police actions we have measured cause a sense of justice which yields compliance. Our models contain error to the extent that preexisting citizen attitudes act as filters of police action and attenuate or enhance the impact of police actions on the likelihood of compliance.

Exploring the middle ground between police action and citizen reaction, that of citizen perception, is necessary to form a more complete picture of citizen responses. One mechanism for developing such research is the use of surveys and vignettes to elicit interpretations of police actions. Research subjects could be drawn from a pool of potential police suspects (a broad cross section of citizens, if one considers traffic enforcement as a mechanism for eligibility in that pool) and important attitudes that shape judgments about police would be measured. Subsequently a vignette would be offered as a stimulus (police actions could be systematically altered in the vignettes to establish randomly varying stimuli) to which citizens would report their perceptions and perhaps self-report their imagined response to the police stimuli if a compliance request is made. This is a simplified summary of a significant future research agenda, which would illuminate the area between procedural justice research (Tyler, 1990; Lind and Tyler 1988) and the present research. The former measures perceptions and outcomes, the latter measures actions and outcomes, and the proposed agenda attempts to link the three together.

Recasting the Project on Policing Neighborhoods to capture more specific data regarding police actions and citizen responses is also a viable research strategy. Much of the data collected by the POPN researchers could be collected by the observers, rather than coded from narratives. Training observers to this end, and fielding a research project is necessary to replicate the results found from coding data from observers' narratives. In addition, such a research agenda would help refine the theoretical statements generated in the course of this research.

In combination, a researcher could field an observation project to collect data on police-citizen interactions, with particular focus on compliance situations. After an observation period in which the names of compliance targets and systematic observation data are collected, compliance targets could be followed up with a telephone survey assessing their perceptions of police action and their response. This would enable researchers to determine what citizens attended to in the course of the encounter and measure the relative importance or weight that citizens give to different police actions during their decision making. Such research would further aid in isolating specific police actions to which citizens are attuned when making decisions to comply. It would also assist in establishing what the base level of citizen compliance might be under certain circumstances and how coercion, just action, and third parties influence the likelihood of compliance.

Overall, the focus of future research must be to fill in the link between citizens' preexisting attitudes, authority actions, citizen perceptions of actions, and citizens' behaviors in response to authority actions. This research has generated a link, if tenuous, between authority action and citizen response. The psychological mechanisms that are in operation in this decision-making process, however, require further inquiry to establish a more complete model of citizen compliance.

NOTES

INTRODUCTION THROUGH CHAPTER EIGHT

Introduction

[1]Tyler and Kerstetter (1994) note that this particular dimension of police-citizen encounters is in flux. Community-oriented policing is an attempt to return to a halcyon age when the police-citizen relationship was not a transient one. A department's commitment to community-oriented policing would likely directly affect this dimension.

[2] It is conceivable that a nation would involuntarily enter into a treaty to end a conflict, and that a patient suffering a grievous injury would involuntarily submit to a doctor's care. It seems, however, that voluntary forms of interaction are more prevalent in both domains.

[3] McIver and Parks (1983) use citizen emotional state as a dependent variable in their analysis. Beyond this exception, however, there is a dearth of literature examining citizen behavior as an outcome of these interactions.

CHAPTER 1

[1] McCluskey et al. (1999) noted the initial level of an officer's request for compliance as either authoritative or nonauthoritative, but it was not a significant predictor of citizen compliance. This differs from an "entry" tactic because the request for compliance could occur at entry, during processing, or at exit. Hence the level of request examined in that research would be more appropriately considered the entry tactic to the compliance game, not the entry tactic used for the overall police-citizen encounter.

[2]Of importance here is discriminating between the "law in action" and the "law on the books". A citizen is not necessarily attuned to the nuances of the legal codes, but is likely to be influenced by an officer's on the spot evaluation of liability. Further, arrest is more salient punishment than a distant and uncertain penalty that may accompany official processing.

[3]An alternative conception of gender dyads could be based on normative behavior in gender dyads. Such an approach would predict that etiquette norms might control male citizens' behavior in encounters with females (Tedeschi and Felson, 1994).

[4]Regardless of the definition or conception accepted this constellation of behaviors is marked by instability and unpredictability (in varying degrees) in discharging everyday tasks. Thus, the mentally ill citizen is disadvantaged by not being able to follow the script that would guide two rational calculators.

[5]Markowitz and Tedeschi (1998) make an argument about the relationship between SES and violence that is similar to this criticism of conflict theory. Since the linkage between SES and violence lacks a mechanism for agency the

authors argue that attitudes towards "disputatiousness" might intervene. Similarly, we argue that conflict theory requires some mediating explanatory mechanism to link subject characteristics and behavioral responses. Our usage of demographic characteristics reflects an imperfect proxy for attitudes which mediate outcomes.

CHAPTER 2

[1]Note that the use of "disrespect" in previous analyses includes both passive and active disrespect (ignoring versus cursing, for example), which arguably produce differing reactions in the target (Mastrofski, Reisig, and McCluskey, 2002). In hypotheses below, we note that ignoring a citizen is a violation of their "voice," thus; disrespect will require respecification as a measure under the present framework to avoid double counting its potential effect. It is also important to note that a citizen's previous attitudes toward and beliefs about police may shape how they interpret acts, and so the characteristics with which these are associated might be predictive of outcomes.

[2]Miller (1977) notes that police legitimacy emanates from personal and impersonal authority. Community policing is an attempt to abandon impersonal professionalism for the halcyon tradition of personal treatment. Kerstetter and Tyler (1994) indicate that *personal* authority draws upon the individual's sense that the authority is ethical and benevolent.

[3]We argue that the context within which social interactions occur is important for assessing the likelihood of a compliant outcome. A general overview of the literature on contextual factors indicates that they influence criminal justice decisions by judges as well as police (Myers and Talarico, 1986; Smith, 1986). This argument revisits the nature of our dependent variable. Both Warner (1997) and Smith (1986) are interested in police actions, we are examining citizen actions and the effects that context exerts on those individuals.

[4]This literature also suggests interactions between the ecological context of the police-citizen encounters and the predictive power of coercive factors, procedural justice perceptions, and citizen irrationality. Despite the plausible existence of these interactions our focus will remain on the dependent variable: do citizens comply, or do they rebel? The phenomenon in question, in our opinion, has not been analyzed so thoroughly that we can confidently offer hypotheses regarding interactions across levels of analysis.

[5]Control and Strain explanations are included separately since the two have differing assumptions about human nature. Control theory argues that our deviant desires are bound by the social structure and, in contrast, strain theory posits that the social structure acts as a push toward deviance. Control reflects assumptions about human nature consistent with Freud and Hobbes–a selfish

malefactor in need of restraint, but Strain's starting assumption has a more benign view of human nature.

CHAPTER 3

[1]This index is similar to that used by the Project on Human Development in Chicago Neighborhoods to measure neighborhood conditions (Sampson et al. 1997).

[2]An encounter was defined as police-citizen contact lasting more than one minute, involving three verbal exchanges between the observed officer and citizen, or any situation where an officer made physical contact with a citizen. Encounters that lasted less than a minute, involved less than three exchanges, and in which no physical contact was made were not considered for this investigation.

CHAPTER 4

[1] One should note that the author is not an "inexperienced coder" as defined in this text, and the first 40 cases in the data are not subject to the same criticism. The author has hand coded several hundred cases from the data set on various projects involving these data.

CHAPTER 5

[1] The 83 missing cases can be compared on the coded data provided by POPN observers. These cases had a higher reported rate of "global" non-compliance, which summarized the citizen's behavior across the entire encounter (nearly 28 percent) than the observers reported in the remainder of cases (eighteen percent). This is of some concern since the difference is statistically significant ($x^2=4.36$, 1 d.f., $p < .05$) across those missing data and those cases for which data are coded. A partial explanation for the difference is that data cleaning of cases with limited narrative data is impossible, so the cases in our "missing" pool represent cases with a larger coding error rate. This is one possible explanation for the higher rate of noncompliance in that portion of the sample.

[2] Our unconventional treatment of gender, in the form of a variable measuring the dyad between the lead officer and the target may raise concerns as to whether this variable is properly operationalized. Separate models using officer gender and target gender are essentially identical to those presented here. Furthermore, a model of citizen compliance using officer gender and citizen gender fails to pass chi-square test when those two predictors are included in a model ($x^2=5.14$, 2 d.f. $p > .07$) of our dependent variable.

[3] An alternative coding scheme to the one proposed would be to make indexes of legitimacy enhancers (respect, information seeking, voice, leniency, independence) and legitimacy attenuators (disrespect, termination of voice, bias). We created two variables that accomplish that and ran models, not fully reported here, substituting those two indexes for the three procedural justice indexes. The index of legitimacy enhancing actions was significant, and for every one unit increase in that variable the likelihood of compliance increased 1.5 times. Similarly, the index of legitimacy attenuating actions was significant, and for every unit increase in that variable the likelihood of compliance decreased 1.7 times.

CHAPTER 6

[1] Related to this argument is the notion that requests for identification occur very early in police-citizen interactions. This limits the variation and potential importance of pre-request dynamics when one limits the study of compliance to whether citizens cooperate with requests for identification.

CHAPTER 7

[1] Relatives who are adversaries are included in the adversary category, they have not been altogether excluded from the analysis.

[2] Hosmer and Lemeshow (1989: 69) argue for models with a set interaction terms in a fully interactive model as an alternative to splitting the sample. Similar inferences were drawn when we used this method. Interaction terms for the adversary and neighborhood disadvantage models produce x^2 change statistics that indicated those models offered no better prediction than a simple main effects model. The irrationality and probable cause models, mirrored the results presented in the split sample models. The x^2 change statistics were significant and the same interaction terms were significant in those two models.

APPENDIX
Coding Rules

There are several threshold issues that were addressed in developing a coding scheme in the accompanying research. The first two require establishing the limits of entry tactics and how they should be coded for police and citizens. The third is when it is determined that phase II has begun in an encounter.

A. Entry tactics for police represent the FIRST action that police take in the course of the encounter and are measured with a series of dummy variable actions described below (derived from Mastrofski, Snipes, and Supina 1996).

B. Entry tactics for the citizens represent the FIRST action or response (not non-compliance or disrespect) and are coded only prior to any police action. In the original draft of the coding rules we considered measuring this during phase I and phase II. Reevaluation prompted us to measure this as an entry tactic so that it would not be caused by a police action. The concern is that citizen "morality" might be a reaction to tactics if measured during the phases, and not an indicator of some predisposition toward granting legitimacy to police. By restricting it to an entry tactic we remove the influence of police action on observed citizen actions.

C. The second phase of an encounter occurs once the citizen responds to or ignores the FIRST compliance request made by the police. Ignoring officer requests is considered present when the police take an action after the compliance request or the citizen takes an action after the compliance request but the compliance request remained unaddressed.

RULES FOR CODING INDICATORS

Entry Tactics

Police Entry Tactics
These are coded in the following six dummy categories with zero representing the absence of the tactic:

1 = passive (just listening to a citizen on scene)
2 = ask questions
3 = issue command
4 = issue threat
5 = physical force - includes contact with person or brandishing a weapon
6 = police have citizen under arrest

Citizen Entry Tactics
This is only coded if citizen action precedes any police action/stimulus to ensure that citizen behavior is not a response to police behavior. This is essentially an indicator of "morality" of police presence. Two dummy variables are coded in the following format:

0 = no indication, or police have first action during the encounter
1 = citizen makes positive verbalization regarding police presence
0 = no indication, or police have first action during the encounter
1 = citizen makes negative verbalization regarding police presence

Phase I Coding

All Phase I actions were coded prior to the first request for compliance; also, language used to describe coding conventions is adopted within these directions to maintain consistency with the POPN coders.

Procedural Justice Variables

Phase I Ethicality
This variable captures the quality of police-citizen interaction in terms of respectful and disrespectful treatment. Police actions such as responsiveness to citizen requests and indications of polite tones are coded as 1. Disrespectful actions are coded as 2, and capture active

forms of disrespect by police towards citizens. The following actions are considered disrespectful when performed by the police:

To qualify as "disrespectful" the police must do something that shows disrespect to the individual. This can include a variety of verbal statements: calling the citizen names, making derogatory statements about the citizen or his family, making disparaging or belittling remarks, slurs (racial, sexual, lifestyle).

Certain gestures and actions are to be coded as disrespectful. "Flipping the bird" (displaying the 3rd finger in the direction of the citizen), obscene gestures, etc.

Shouting at citizens, except in cases of emergency, also constitutes disrespectful behavior.

If both respectful and disrespectful acts occur during phase one then it was coded as 3.

0 = neither respect nor disrespect present
1 = respectful treatment present
2 = disrespectful treatment present
3 = both respectful and disrespectful treatment present

Phase I Voice Effects
If the citizen presented an explanation to the police, regarding the presenting situation, then this was coded as 1. If the citizen did not present an explanation to the police then this is coded as 0.

If the police ignored a citizen's explanation, interrupted them while they were telling their side of a story, or ordered them to be silent during Phase I then code this variable 1. If there is no evidence of authoritative termination of voice then code this variable 0.

Phase I Seeking Information
If the police asked the citizen about their behavior and its relationship to a legal standard, or asked them to clarify their actions, or asked them to explain what has happened at the scene code this variable as 1. If there is no evidence of the police actively seeking clarification or information on the scene then code this variable as 0.

Coding of three different types of information seeking by the police is captured:

P1PSINF1 = seek information regarding the identity of the individual
P1PSINF2 = seek information about the presenting situation
P1PSINF3 = seek information about how the situation can be resolved

Phase I Evidence of Police Bias
This variable is coded as 1 if the police tell the citizen that another citizen is guiding the decision making of the officer during the encounter. This would include statements such as: "X thinks it would be good for you to leave for the night" or "...your neighbor asked me to come over and tell you to turn down your stereo." If there is no evidence that the police based their decision on the preferences of a citizen at the scene then this variable is coded as zero.

Phase I Evidence of Police Independence
This variable is coded as 1 if the police tell the citizen that their decision making on the scene is affected by legal standards. This would include mentioning that curfew laws are being enforced, or that a citizen has a court order against them and this is influencing the officer's decision making. If there is no evidence of that the police based their decision on legal standards then this variable is coded as zero.

Phase I Evidence of Police Independence
This variable is coded as a 1, if the police mention that their behavior or words indicate whether the police tell the citizen that they are "giving them a break" or "going easy" on them in the present situation by taking less punitive action against them than the law allows or than they could otherwise engage in (for example, in cases with juveniles they may note that they will not inform parents). Otherwise, absent such indication it is coded as zero.

Phase I Evidence (Probable Cause) Level
Is a measure of probable cause. The following scale is used to generate probable cause indicator when the number is greater than or equal to 2. When the evidence level rises to two or above we code 1 on evidence, if the evidence level does not rise above Probable Cause then evidence is coded as 0.

The following scale, developed by Mastrofski et al., (1996) measures evidence components as follows:

officer observes violation (2), officer obtains physical evidence implicating citizen (2), officer hears full confession (2), officer hears eyewitness testimony implicating citizen (1), officer hears partial confession (1). This evidence scale is expected to be positively related to the likelihood of compliance.

Coercion variables

Phase I Suggestions
Verbal negotiation and persuasion and requests of the citizen are coded as 1. This is passive verbal communication with the target. If there is no evidence of this condition present then a 0 is coded.

Phase I Commands
Stern verbal requests made of the target is coded as 1. This is indicated by a note that the statement was a command, or that it was made in a loud authoritative tone. If there is no evidence of this condition present then a 0 is coded.

Phase I Threats
This would be coded 1 when the police make it clear that there is a potential physical or legal consequence for disobedience such as forcing the citizen to leave or behave with physical effort. If there is no evidence of this condition present then a 0 is coded.

Phase I Mention of Arrests or Citations
This is coded 1 if the police mention that the behavior they observe in the encounter is arrestable or citeable. Threats of arrest or citation are considered mentions of arrest or citation. If there is no evidence of this condition present then a 0 is coded. Citations are coded as a 2 to discern that type of sanction from an arrest. When both are present then the code is 3.

0=no mention
1=mentioned arrest
2=mentioned citation
3=mentioned both arrest and citation

Phase I Handcuffing
This is coded 1 if the police apply handcuffs to a citizen. If there is no evidence of this condition present then a 0 is coded.

Phase I Searching
This is coded 1 if the police search the person, the area immediately surrounding the person, or pat down for weapons. If there is no evidence of this condition present then a 0 is coded.

Phase I Physical Force
This is coded 1 if the police use a firm grip, pain compliance technique, impact method, or brandish a weapon in citizen presence. If there is no evidence of this condition present then a 0 is coded.

Phase I Arrest
This is coded 1 if the police arrest the citizen (i.e., make it clear they will be processed on formal charges). If there is no evidence of this condition present then a 0 is coded.

Phase I Citation
This is coded 1 if the police write a citation out for the target citizen. If there is no evidence of this condition present then a 0 is coded.

Phase I Citizen Weapon This is coded as 1 if the citizen possesses a gun, knife, or other offensive object (baseball bat) within reach. If there is no evidence of this condition present then a 0 is coded.

Phase I Type of Officer Request Issued (Specific to behavioral compliance requests)
This represents the type of requested made by the police, in a two digit format: The first digit corresponds to whether the request is a suggestion or asked (1) or whether there is a command or threat to perform the task (2) the second digit corresponds to the following request types:

1 = request to leave scene
2 = request to leave person alone
3 = request to cease disorderly behavior
4 = request to cease illegal behavior

Third Party Variables

Third Party Positive Verbal
This is coded when there is a third party present and they offer POSITIVE verbal support for the police prior to the initial request for compliance. This is characterized by statements that indicate the 3rd party supports the police's intervention in the encounter. This could include, but not be restricted to, "Glad you are here." "Thank you for coming." Etc.

0= no evidence of third party positive verbal support
1= evidence of third party positive verbal support

Third Party Negative Verbal
This is coded when there is a third party present and they offer NEGATIVE verbal support for the police prior to the initial request for compliance. This is characterized by statements that indicate the 3rd party questions the police's intervention in the encounter. This could include, but not be restricted to, "We don't need you here." "This is our business." Etc.

In addition, disrespectful acts by a third party would be coded as Negative Verbal action. To capture third party disrespectful behavior we adopt a modified version of POPN's definition of disrespectful behavior:

The standard for disrespectful behavior we apply will be independent of anything the officer says or does about whether the citizen showed or failed to show respect to which the officer felt entitled.

To qualify as "yes," the citizen must do something or fail to do something that shows disrespect to the individual or the authority of the police officer. This can include a variety of verbal statements: calling the officer names, making derogatory statements about the officer or his family, making disparaging or belittling remarks, slurs (racial, sexual, lifestyle). Ignoring the officer's commands or questions also constitutes disrespect.

If the citizen is argumentative, the citizen may or may not be disrespectful, depending on how it was done. If the citizen disagrees with the officer or questions/objects to his actions--but does so in a polite way will NOT code the citizen as disrespectful. However, if the citizen disagrees with the officer by speaking loudly or interrupting the officer, then code this as disrespectful.

Certain gestures and actions are to be coded as disrespectful. "Flipping the bird" (displaying the 2nd finger in the direction of the police), obscene gestures, spitting in the presence of an officer (even if not in the direction of the officer) (Mastrofski et al., 1997).

0 = no evidence of 3rd party negative verbal remarks
1= evidence of 3rd party negative verbal remarks

Third Party Rebellion
Third party rebellion is coded if the police make a compliance request of another citizen involved in the encounter and two variables capture whether a compliant or rebellious citizen was present:

0 = no non-compliant citizen present
1 = citizen was noncompliant
0 = no compliant citizen present
1 = compliant citizen present

Third Party Adversary
Third party adversary is a dummy variable coded 1 when a person is present who has a grievance or a dispute with the target citizen. Victims of crime or disputants in domestic or other arguments are adversaries.

Relative Present
A relative is someone who has a blood tie (mother, brother, sister) or a continuing relationship such as boyfriend-girlfriend with the target. The presence of a relative is coded as a 1, otherwise it is 0.

Relative Adversary (*P13PRADV*):
This is coded as 1 if a person satisfying adversary and relative statuses is present on scene. Otherwise this is coded as 0.

Phase I Citizen Response to Officer Request
This is the response variable for the officer's request for self-control with the following coding categories:

1 = refused
2 = ignored
3 = promised to comply
4 = complied in presence

Identification Compliance Coding

Phase I Type of Officer Request Issued (Specific to ID requests)
For identification question, this represents the type of ID requested:

0=No request apparent [used for determining the cases that should be excluded]
1=Name and number
2=Actual License or ID Card

Phase I Citizen Response to Officer Request
For identification analyses, this represents the following citizen response categories:

0 = did not comply
1 = gave indication that could not comply
2 = told officer name or other information
3 = gave ID as requested

Other Variables

Variables obtained from the POPN observation instrument include the following items derived from raw electronic data and recoded as noted in the text of the book:

Citizen Gender (to be used to create the gender dyad variable)
What is the citizen's sex?

1   male
2   female

Citizen Age
What is the citizen's age?

1   preschool (up to 5 years)
2   child (6-12)
3   young teen (13-17)
4   older teen (18-20)
5   young adult (21-29)
6   adult (30-44)
7   middle-aged (45-59)
8   senior (60 and above)

Citizen Race
What is the citizen's race/ethnicity?

1   white (if white, minority=0; else minority=1)
2   black
3   Hispanic
4   Asian
5   American Indian
6   Other

Citizen Social Class
What was the level of wealth did the citizen appear to have?

1   chronic poverty (homeless, no apparent means of
    support)
2   low (subsistence only)
3   middle
4   above middle

Police Audience
Upon arrival at the scene, how many police officers were
already present?

Citizen Audience
What was the maximum number of citizens (bystanders +
participants) present at any one time during the encounter?

The Elements of Irrationality

Citizen Mentally Ill
Did this citizen show any signs of mental disorder?

1   no
2   yes

Citizen Intoxicated
Did this citizen appear to be under the influence of alcohol
or other drugs?

1   no indication of alcohol/drug use
2   indication of use, but no visible effects on behavior
3   slight behavioral indications (slight speech)
4   strong behavioral indications (strong speech,
    difficulty standing/understanding conversation)
5   unconscious

Citizen Angry/Excited
What best characterizes the citizen's emotional state at the
beginning of the contact?

1   not elevated (calm)
2   elevated--fear or anger
3   elevated--happy
4   depressed--sadness or remorse

The following variables were obtained from POPN's officer survey:

Officer Gender
This is used to create the gender dyad variable.
Officer's sex
        1= male
        2= female

Officer Race
0=no response
1=white (if white minority=0; non-missing else, minority=1).
2=black
3=latino

4=asian
5=other
-6=not applicable
-8=refused
-9=don't know

PHASE II CODING

Phase II coding conventions follow those outlined above. It is important to note that phase II begins AFTER the police ask a target for compliance and they are ignored, rejected, promised that compliance is forthcoming, or the person complies in presence of the police. Phase II coding represents only those police or citizen actions that follow the citizen's phase I response. Situational conditions such as evidence, adversaries, and relatives present are only coded if their status changes. For example, if adversaries appear in phase II they are coded as present for phase II.

Phase 2 Entry Tactic
This represents the officer's first counter move to citizen's response or the first move of police subsequent to citizen compliance response. It is a compound coding representing passive, verbal or physical responses in the first digit. Second digits represent the level of the entry tactic as noted below in parentheses:

0=passive (wait, talk to others on scene)
1=verbal (1)=suggest (2) request (3) command (4) threaten physical (5) threaten legal
2=physical (1)=search (2) handcuff (3) physical force (4) arrest (5) cite

(n.b., that verbatim POPN items, and directions for disrespect were drawn directly from the training and field manuals prepared by the research team, cited below.)

Mastrofski, Stephen D. et al. 1997. Patrol Officer Observation
        Notebook for the Project on Policing Neighborhoods.
        Michigan State University: East Lansing, MI.

REFERENCES

Anderson, E. 1999. *Code of the Streets.* New York: Norton.

Arendt, H. 1973. *On Violence.* New York: Harcourt, Brace, and World.

Azjen, I. 1987. "Attitudes, Traits, and Actions: Dispositional Prediction of Behavior in Personality and Social Psychology." *Advances in Experimental and Social Psychology,* 20: 1-63.

Back, K. 1983. "Compliance and Conformance in an Age of Sincerity." In M. Rosenbaum (ed.) *Compliant Behavior.* New York: Human Science Press.

Bayley, D. H. 1986. "The Tactical Choices of Police Patrol Officers." *Journal of Criminal Justice,* 14: 329-48.

Bayley, D. H. 1998. *What Works in Policing.* New York: Oxford.

Bayley, D. H. & E. Bittner. 1984. "Learning the Skills of Policing." *Law and Contemporary Problems,* 47: 35-59.

Berk, S. F. & D. R. Loseke. 1980-1. "'Handling' Family Violence: Situational Determinants of Police Arrest in Domestic Disturbances." *Law & Society Review,* 15: 167-77.

Bittner, E. 1970. *The Functions of Police in Modern Society.* Washington DC: United States Government Printing Office.

Black, D. J. 1980. *The Manners and Customs of the Police.* New York: Academic Press.

Black, D. J. 1993. *The Social Structure of Right and Wrong.* San Diego: Academic Press.

Black, D. J. 1995. "The Epistemology of Pure Sociology." *Law & Social Inquiry.* 20: 829-70.

Blau, P. M. 1967. *Exchange and Power in Social Life.* New York: Wiley.

Braithwaite, J. 1989. *Crime Shame and Reintegration.* New York: Cambridge University Press.

Brehm, J. 1996. "Steps Towards a Political Science of Compliance." A Paper presented at the 54th Annual Meeting of the Midwest Political Science Association, Chicago, IL.

Brown, M. K. 1988. *Working the Street.* New York: Russell Sage.

Bureau of Justice Statistics. 2001. *Contacts Between Police and the Public.* Washington, DC: U.S. Department of Justice.

Casey, J. T. & J. T. Scholz. 1991. "Beyond Deterrence: Behavioral Decision Theory and Tax Compliance." *Law & Society Review,* 25: 821-43.

Cloward, R. A. & L. E. Ohlin. 1960. *Delinquency and Opportunity.* Free Press: Glencoe, IL.

Cohen J. 1960. "A Coefficient of Agreement For Nominal Scales." *Educational and Psychological Measurement,* 20: 37-46.

Cross, A. W., & L. R. Churchill. 1982. "Ethical and Cultural Dimensions of Informed Consent: A Case Study and Analysis." *Annals of Internal Medicine,* 96: 110-13.

Dunford, F., D. Huizinga, & D. Elliott. 1986. "The Role of Arrest in Domestic Assault." *Criminology,* 28: 183-206.

Dunham, R. G. & G. P. Alpert. 1988. "Neighborhood Differences in Attitudes Toward Policing." *Journal of Criminal Law and Criminology,* 79: 504-23.

Durkheim, E. 1893/1956. *The Division of Labor in Society*. New York: Free Press.

Emerson, R. M. 1983. "Holistic Effects in Social Control Decision-Making." *Law & Society Review,* 17: 425-55.

Engle, R. & E. Silver. 2001. "Policing Mentally Disordered Suspects: A Reexamination of the Criminalization Hypothesis." *Criminology,* 39: 225-52.

Erez, E. 1984. "Self-defined 'Desert' and Citizens' Assessment of the Police." *Journal of Criminal Law and Criminology,* 75: 1276-99.

Ericson, Richard V. 1982. *Reproducing Order: A Study of Police Patrol Work*. Toronto: U of Toronto Press.

Fox, J. 1991. *Regression Diagnostics*. Thousand Oaks, CA: Sage.

French, J. & B. Raven. 1959. "The Basis of Social Power." In D. Cartwright (ed.) *Studies in Social Power*. Ann Arbor, MI: Institute for Social Research.

Gibbs, J. P. 1981. *Norms, Deviance, and Social Control: Conceptual Matters*. New York: Elsevier.

Gibbs, J. P. 1989. *Control*. Urbana, IL: U of Illinois Press.

Gilligan, C. 1982. *In a Different Voice*. Cambridge, MA: Harvard University Press.

Goffman, E. 1959. *The Presentation of Self in Everyday Life*. New York: Doubleday Anchor.

Goldstein, A. P. 1994. *The Ecology of Aggression*. Plenum: NY.

Gottfredson, M. R. & D. M. Gottfredson. 1988. *Decision-making in Criminal Justice*. New York: Plenum.

Gurr, T. R. 1970. *Why Men Rebel*. Princeton, NJ: Princeton University Press.

Hagan, J.& C. Albonetti. 1982. "Race, Class, and the Perception of Criminal Injustice in America." *American Journal of Sociology,* 88: 329-55.

Hawkins, K. 1983. "Bargain and Bluff: Compliance Strategy and Deterrence in the Enforcement of Regulation." *Law and Policy Quarterly.* 5: 35-73.

Henkin, L. 1979. *How Nations Behave.* New York: Columbia University Press.

Hirschi, T. 1969. *Causes of Delinquency.* Berkeley: University of California Press.

Homans, G. C. 1961. *Social Behavior: Its Elementary Forms.* New York: Harcourt, Brace and World.

Hosmer, D. & S. Lemeshow. 1989. *Applied Logistic Regression.* New York: Wiley.

Hudson, J. 1970. "Police-Citizen Encounters That Lead to Citizen Complaints." *Social Problems,* 18: 179-93.

Katz, J. 1988. *Seductions of Crime: Moral and Sensual Attractions of Doing Evil.* New York: Basic Books.

Kelman, H. C. 1958. "Compliance, Identification, and Internalization Three Processes of Attitude Change." *Journal of Conflict Resolution,* 2: 51-60.

Kerner, O. 1968. *Report of the National Advisory Commission on Civil Disorders.* New York: E. P. Dutton & Co.

Klepper, S. & D. Nagin. 1989. "Tax Compliance and Perceptions of the Risks of Detection and Criminal Prosecution." *Law & Society Review,* 23: 209-39.

Klinger, D. 1994. "Demeanor or Crime? Why 'Hostile' Citizens are More Likely to be Arrested." *Criminology,* 32: 475-93.

Klinger, D. 1997. "The Negotiated Order of Police Work: An
    Ecological Theory of Police Response to Deviance."
    Criminology, 35: 277-306.

Klockars, C. 1984. "Blue Lies and Police Placebos: The Moralities of
    Police Lying." *American Behavioral Scientist,* 27: 529-44.

Kornhauser, R. D. 1978. *Social Sources of Delinquency.* Chicago: U of
    Chicago Press.

Krohn, M. 1986. "The Web of Conformity: A Network Approach to the
    Explanation of Delinquent Behavior." *Social Problems,* 33: 81-
    93.

Lambert, E. 2003. "The Impact of Organizational Justice on
    Correctional Staff." *Journal of Criminal Justice,* 31: 155-68.

Landis, J. & Koch, G. G. 1977. "The Measurement of Observer
    Agreement for Categorical Data. *Biometrics,* 33: 159-74.

Lane, R. 1988. "Procedural Goods in a Democracy: How One is
    Treated Versus What One Gets." *Social Justice Research,* 2:
    177-92.

Lanza-Kaduce, L. & R. G. Greenleaf. 1994. "Police-Citizen
    Encounters: Turk on Norm Resistance." *Justice Quarterly* 11:
    605-24.

Leventhal, G. S. 1980. "What Should Be Done with Equity Theory?" In
    K.J. Gergen, M.S. Greenberg, & R.H. Weiss (eds.) *Social
    Exchange: Advances in Theory and Research.* New York:
    Plenum Press.

Lind, E. A. & T. R. Tyler. 1988. *The Social Psychology of Procedural
    Justice.* Plenum: New York.

Long, J. S. 1997. *Regression Models for Categorical and Limited
    Dependent Variables.* Thousand Oaks, CA: Sage.

Luckenbill, D. F. & D. P. Doyle. 1989. "Structural Position and
   Violence: Developing a Cultural Explanation." *Criminology,*
   27:801-18.

Makkai, T. & J. Braithwaite. 1994. "Reintegrative Shaming and
   Compliance with Regulatory Standards." *Criminology,* 32: 361-
   86.

Manning, Peter 1977. *Police Work.* Cambridge, MA: MIT Press.

Markowitz, F. E. & R. B. Felson. 1998. "Social-Demographic Attitudes
   and Violence." *Criminology,* 36: 117-38.

Masters, J.C., Felleman, E.S., & Barden, R.C. 1981. "Experimental
   Studies of Affective States in Children." In B. Lahey & A. E.
   Kazdin (eds.) *Advances in Clinical Child Psychology.* New
   York: Plenum.

Mastrofski, S. D. 1999. *Policing for People.* Washington, D.C.: Police
   Foundation.

Mastrofski, S. D., R. B. Parks, A. J. Reiss, Jr., & R. E. Worden. 1997.
   *Patrol Officer Observation Notebook for the Project on Policing
   Neighborhoods.* Michigan State University: East Lansing, MI.

Mastrofski, S. D., R. B. Parks, A. J. Reiss, Jr., R. E. Worden, C.
   DeJong, J. B. Snipes, & W. Terrill. 1998. *Systematic
   Observation of Public Police: Applying Field Research Methods
   to Policy Issues.* Washington, DC: National Institute of Justice.

Mastrofski, S. D., M. D. Reisig, & J. D. McCluskey. 2002. "Police
   Disrespect Toward the Public: An Encounter-Based Analysis."
   Criminology, 40: 515-51.

Mastrofski, S. D., J. B. Snipes, R. B. Parks, & C. D. Maxwell. 2000.
   "The Helping Hand of the Law: Police Control of Citizens on
   Request." *Criminology,* 38: 307-42.

Mastrofski, S. D., J. B. Snipes, & A. E. Supina. 1996. "Compliance on Demand: The Public's Response to Specific Police Requests." *Journal of Research in Crime and Delinquency,* 33: 269-305.

Mastrofski, Stephen D., R. E. Worden, & J. B. Snipes. 1995. "Law Enforcement in a Time of Community Policing." *Criminology,* 33: 539-63.

McCluskey, J. D. & S. D. Mastrofski. 1997. "Police-Citizen Cooperation in Everyday Encounters." Paper presented at the 49th Annual Meeting of the American Society of Criminology: San Diego, CA.

McCluskey, J. D., S. D. Mastrofski, & R. B. Parks. 1999. "To Acquiesce or Rebel: Predicting Citizen Compliance with Police Requests." *Police Quarterly,* 2: 389-416.

McEwen, C. A. & R. J. Maiman. 1984. "Mediation in Small Claims Court: Achieving Compliance Through Consent." *Law & Society Review,* 18: 9-49.

McIver, J. P. & R. B. Parks. 1983. "Evaluating Police Performance: Identification of Effective and Ineffective Police Actions." in R. R. Bennett (ed.), *Police at Work: Policy Issues and Analysis.* Beverly Hills, CA: Sage.

Meichenbaum, D. & Gilmore, J.B. 1984. "The Nature of Unconscious Processes: A Cognitive-behavioral Perspective." In K. Bowers & D. Meichenbaum (eds.) *The Unconscious Reconsidered.* New York: Wiley.

Menard, S. 1995. *Applied Logistic Regression Analysis.* Thousand Oaks, CA: Sage.

Menard, S. & D. Elliott. 1994. "Delinquent Bonding, Moral Beliefs, and Illegal Behavior: A Three-Wave Panel Model." *Justice Quarterly,* 11: 173-88.

Merton, R. K. 1968. *Social Theory and Social Structure.* New York: Free Press.

Milgram, S. 1973. *Obedience to Authority.* New York: Harper & Row.

Miller, W. R. 1977. *Cops and Bobbies: Police Authority in New York and London, 1830-1870.* Chicago: University of Chicago Press.

Molm, L. 1997. *Coercive Power in Social Exchange.* New York: Cambridge University Press.

Mongrain, S., & L. Standing. 1989. "Impairment of Cognition, Risk-taking, and Self-perception by Alcohol." *Perceptual and Motor Skills*, 69: 199-210.

Morenoff, J., R. Sampson, S. Raudenbush. 2002. "Neighborhood Inequality, Collective Efficacy, and the Spatial Dynamics of Urban Violence." *Criminology,* 39: 517-59.

Muir, W. K., Jr. 1977. *Police: Streetcorner Politicians.* Chicago: University of Chicago Press.

Myers, M. A. & S. M. Talarico. 1986 "The Social Contexts of Racial Discrimination in Sentencing." *Social Problems*, 33: 236-51.

Novak, K. J., J. Frank, B. Smith, & R. Engle. 2002. "Revisiting the Decision to Arrest: Comparing Beat and Community Officers." *Crime & Delinquency,* 48: 70-98.

Paoline, E. A. Forthcoming, 2003. "Taking Stock: Toward a Richer Understanding of Police Culture." *Journal of Criminal Justice.*

Patchin, M. 1988. *Resolving Disputes Between Nations: Coercion or Conciliation?* Durham: Duke University Press.

Paternoster, R., R. Bachman, R. Brame, & L. W. Sherman. 1997. "Do Fair Procedures Matter? The Effect of Procedural Justice on Spouse Assault." *Law & Society Review,* 31: 163-204.

Paternoster, R., Brame, R., Mazzerolle, P., & Piquero, A. 1998. "Using the Correct Statistical Test For the Equality of Regression Coefficients." *Criminology,* 36: 859-66.

Patterson, G. R., J. B. Reid, & T. Dishion. 1992. *Antisocial Boys.* Eugene, OR:Castalia.

Pendelton, D. 1983. "Doctor-Patient Communication: A Review." In D. Pendelton & J. Hasler (eds.) *Doctor-Patient Communication* New York: Academic Press.

Pernanen, K. 1991. *Alcohol in Human Violence.* New York: Guilford.

Plato. 1992. *Republic.* In M. Morgan (ed.). *Classics of Moral and Political Theory.* Indianapolis, IN: Hackett.

Rawls, J. 1971. *A Theory of Justice.* Cambridge, MA: Belknap Press.

Reisig, M. D., J. D. McCluskey, S. D. Mastrofski, & W. Terrill. 2003. "Culture, Situation, or Context? Explaining Citizen Disrespect of the Police." Unpublished Manuscript, East Lansing, MI: Michigan State University, School of Criminal Justice.

Reisig, M. D. & R. B. Parks. 2001. "Experience, Quality of Life, and Neighborhood Context." *Justice Quarterly,* 17: 607-30.

Reiss, A. J., Jr. 1971. *The Police and the Public.* New Haven, CT: Yale University Press.

Reiss, A. J., Jr. 1984. "Consequences of Compliance and Deterrence Models of Law Enforcement For the Exercise of Police Discretion." *Law and Contemporary Problems,* 47: 84-122.

Riksheim, E. & S. Chermak. 1993. "Causes of Police Behavior Revisited." *Journal of Criminal Justice,* 21: 353-82.

Sampson, R. J. & D. J. Bartusch. 1998. "Legal Cynicism and (Subcultural?) Tolerance of Deviance: The Neighborhood Context of Racial Differences." *Law & Society Review,* 32: 777-804.

Sampson, R. J. & W. B. Groves. 1989. "Community Structure and Crime: Testing Social Disorganization Theory." *American Journal of Sociology,* 94: 774-802.

Sampson, R. J., S. W. Raudenbush, & F. Earls. 1997. "Neighborhoods and Violent Crime: A Multilevel Study of Collective Efficacy." *Science,* 277: 918-24.

Scheff, T. J. & S. M. Retzinger. 1991. *Emotions and Violence.* Lexington, MA: D. C. Heath and Company.

Scholz, J. & N. Pinney. 1995. "Duty, Fear, and Tax Compliance: The Heuristic Basis of Citizenship Behavior." *American Journal of Political Science,* 39: 490-512.

Shaw, C.R. & H. D. McKay. 1942. *Juvenile Delinquency in Urban Areas.* Chicago: University of Chicago Press.

Sherman, L. W. 1993. "Defiance, Deterrence, and Irrelevance: A Theory of the Criminal Sanction." *Journal of Research in Crime and Delinquency,* 30: 445-73.

Sherman, L. W., & R. W. Berk. 1984. "The Specific Deterrent Effects of Arrest on Domestic Assault." *American Sociological Review,* 23: 117-44.

Skolnick, J. H. 1966. *Justice Without Trial: Law Enforcement in Democratic Society.* New York: John Wiley.

Smith, D. A. 1986. "The Neighborhood Context of Police Behavior." In A.J. Reiss Jr. & M. Tonry (eds.) *Communities and Crime.* Chicago: University of Chicago Press.

Smith D. A. & C. A. Visher. 1981. "Street-Level Justice: Situational Determinants of Police Arrest Decisions," *Social Problems,* 29: 167-77.

Stalans, L. J. & M. A. Finn. 1995. "How Novice and Experienced Officers Interpret Wife Assaults: Normative and Efficiency Frames." *Law and Society Review,* 29: 287-321.

Steele, B. F.,& Southwick, L. 1985. "Alcohol and Social Behavior: 1. The Psychology of Drunken Excess." *Journal of Personality and Social Psychology,* 48: 18-34.

Sykes, R. E. & E. E. Brent. 1980. "The Regulation of Interaction by Police: A Systems View of 'Taking Charge.'" *Criminology*, 18: 182-197.

Sykes, R. E. & E. E. Brent. 1983. *Policing: A Social Behaviorist Perspective*. New Brunswick, NJ: Rutgers University Press.

Sykes, R. E. & J. P. Clark. 1975. "A Theory of Deference Exchange in Police-Civilian Encounters." *American Journal of Sociology*, 81: 584-600.

Tavris, C. 1982. *Anger: The Misunderstood Emotion*. New York: Simon & Schuster.

Tedeschi, J. T. & R. B. Felson 1994. *Violence, Aggression, and Coercive Actions*. Washington DC: American Psychological Association.

Thibaut, J., & L. Walker. 1975. *Procedural Justice: A Psychological Analysis*. Hillsdale, NJ: Erlbaum.

Toch, H. 1969/1984. *Violent Men*. Cambridge, MA: Schenkman Publishing Company.

Turk, A. 1969. *Criminality and Legal Order*. Chicago: Rand McNally.

Tyler, T. R. 1988. "What is Procedural Justice? Criteria Used by Citizens to Assess the Fairness of Legal Procedures." *Law and Society Review*, 22: 103-35.

Tyler, T. R. 1990. *Why People Obey the Law*. New Haven, CT: Yale University Press.

Tyler, T. R. 1997. "Citizen Discontent with Legal Procedures: A Social Science Perspective on Civil Procedure Reform." *American Journal of Comparative Law*, 45: 871-904.

Tyler, T. R. 2001. "Public Trust and Confidence in Legal Authorities." *Behavioral Sciences and the Law*, 19: 215-35.

Tyler, T. R. & P. Degoey. 1996. "Trust in Organizational Authorities."
    In R. M. Kramer & T. R. Tyler (eds.) *Trust in Organizations*.
    London: Sage.

Tyler, T. R. & R. Folger. 1980. "Distributional and Procedural Aspects
    of Satisfaction with Citizen-Police Encounters." *Basic and
    Applied Social Psychology,* 1: 281-292.

Tyler, T. R. & W. Kerstetter. 1994. "Moral Authority in Law and
    Criminal Justice: Some Reflections on Wilson's *The Moral
    Sense."* *Criminal Justice Ethics,* 13: 44-53.

Tyler, T. R., K. A. Rasinski, & N. Spodick. 1985. "Influence of Voice
    on Satisfaction With Leaders: Exploring the Meaning of Process
    Control." *Journal of Personality and Social Psychology,* 48: 72-
    81.

Van Maanen, J. 1978. "The Asshole." In P.K. Manning & J. Van
    Maanen (eds.) *Policing a View from the Street.* Santa Monica,
    CA: Goodyear.

Wagner, K. & L. Moriarty. 2002. "Perceived Fairness of Drug Testing
    Policies: Testing Leventhal's Principles of Procedural Justice."
    American Journal of Criminal Justice, 26: 219-33.

Walker, S. 1992. "Origins of the Contemporary Criminal Justice
    Paradigm." *Justice Quarterly,* 9: 47-76.

Warner, B. D. 1997. "Community Characteristics and the Recording of
    Crime: Police Recording of Citizens' Complaints of Burglary
    and Assault." *Justice Quarterly,* 14: 631-49.

Warner, B. D. & G.L. Pierce. 1993. "Reexamining social
    Disorganization Theory Using Calls to the Police as a Measure
    of Crime." *Criminology,* 26: 695-715.

Westley, W. A. 1970. *Violence and the Police.* Cambridge: MIT Press.

White, R. K. 1968. *Nobody Wanted War: Misperception in Vietnam
    and Other Wars.* Garden City, NY: Doubleday.

Wiley, M. G. & T. L. Hudik. 1974. "Police-Citizen Encounters: A Field Test of Exchange Theory." *Social Problems,* 22: 119-29.

Worden, R. E. 1989. "Situational and Attitudinal Explanations of Police Behavior: A Theoretical Reappraisal and Empirical Assessment." *Law and Society Review,* 23: 667-71.

Worden, R. E. & R. L. Shepard. 1996. "Demeanor, Crime, and Police Behavior: A Reexamination of the Police Services Study." *Criminology,* 34: 83-105.

Worden, R. E., R. L. Shepard, & S. D. Mastrofski. 1996. "On the Meaning and Measurement of Suspects' Demeanor Toward the Police." *Journal of Research in Crime and Delinquency,* 33: 324-32.

Zillmann, D. 1979. *Hostility and Aggression.* Hillsdale, NJ: Erlbaum.

Zillmann, D. 1983. Arousal and Aggression. In R.G. Geen & E. I. Donnerstein (eds.) *Aggression: Theoretical and Empirical Reviews.* San Diego, CA: Academic Press.

INDEX